A Survey of Puerto Ricans on the U.S. Mainland in the 1970s

Kal Wagenheim

Published in cooperation with the
Metropolitan Applied Research Center, Inc.

The Praeger Special Studies program—
utilizing the most modern and efficient book
production techniques and a selective
worldwide distribution network—makes
available to the academic, government, and
business communities significant, timely
research in U.S. and international economic, social, and political development.

A Survey of Puerto Ricans on the U.S. Mainland in the 1970s

PRAEGER SPECIAL STUDIES IN U.S. ECONOMIC, SOCIAL, AND POLITICAL ISSUES

Praeger Publishers   New York   Washington   London

Library of Congress Cataloging in Publication Data

Wagenheim, Kal.
    A survey of Puerto Ricans on the U. S. mainland in
the 1970s.

    (Praeger special studies in U. S. economic, social,
and political issues)
    Includes bibliographical references.
    1. Puerto Ricans in the United States—Economic
conditions.   2.   Puerto Ricans in the United States—
Social conditions.   I.   Title.
E184. P85W33   301. 45'16'87295073   74-30712
ISBN 0-275-05980-4

PRAEGER PUBLISHERS
111 Fourth Avenue, New York, N.Y. 10003, U.S.A.

Published in the United States of America in 1975
by Praeger Publishers, Inc.

Printed in the United States of America

The arrival of each new immigrant group in the United States has been a test of the long-cherished American ideal of equal justice and opportunity for all.

Since World War II, Puerto Ricans have become the major new ethnic group in the Northeast, and have also established growing communities in other parts of the nation.

Because Puerto Ricans come from a Spanish-speaking culture that in many ways is foreign to the mainland, their experience has paralleled that of immigrants from foreign countries. But Puerto Ricans are not "immigrants," because they are not foreigners. As U.S. citizens by birthright, Puerto Ricans who move to the mainland are "migrants," because they have crossed no national boundaries.

Statistics can never adequately portray a people-- their dreams, achievements, and frustrations--but such data can be most useful in sketching a people's situation at a given time in history.

I have tried in this book to survey the dramatic changes in the size and nature of the Puerto Rican community in the past three decades; and to measure such key indexes as population growth and dispersion, income, education, and employment. Comparisons are made with the total U.S. population, with Negoes and other Hispanic groups, and with Puerto Ricans in Puerto Rico. This technique of cross-referencing over a period of decades can be most helpful in determining whether a given ethnic group has improved its way of life or is merely standing still. I have also made comparisons between migrants, who were born in Puerto Rico, and their offspring, who were born on the U.S. mainland, in order to see to what degree the second generation has entered the mainstream of American life.

I have used data from many sources, but the one source that offers readily comparable information over a period of decades is the U.S. Census Bureau. Its reports are challenged (with justification) as having underestimated the true size of the U.S. Puerto Rican community, but, at worst, these reports offer an invaluable sample of Puerto Ricans on the mainland.

A few of the highlights of this survey are:

• Official figures mask the true picture of unemployment among U.S. Puerto Ricans, which approaches 33 percent, compared with a nationwide U.S. figure of about 6 percent.

• In the decade 1960-70, the birthrate (for the first time) contributed more to population growth among U.S. Puerto Ricans than did the arrival of new migrants from the island.

• At some point in the 1980s, the number of Puerto Ricans on the U.S. mainland may be as large as the number of Puerto Ricans on the island of Puerto Rico.

• Educational levels for U.S. Puerto Ricans are lower than those for black and white Americans, partly due to a severe (and unjustifiable) shortage of bilingual teachers.

• Puerto Ricans have made significant gains in some socioeconomic areas, but in one crucial category--income-- they lag far behind; and, in relative terms, during the 1960s (the time of the so-called War on Poverty) they did not advance at all.

• There is a growing dichotomy between the achievement levels of migrants and those of U.S.-born Puerto Ricans (the latter have higher levels of education and income, but remain far poorer than the average American).

• Rapidly shrinking job opportunities in urban areas of the U.S. Northeast--particularly for unskilled and semi-skilled males--indicate that Puerto Ricans face a grim struggle for economic survival in the coming decade.

These are just a few of the conclusions reached in this survey, which views U.S. Puerto Ricans on a nation-wide basis. In the course of gathering my data, I also accumulated a considerable amount of additional information about Puerto Ricans in various states and cities on the mainland. Although this material is less complete, I believe it is quite useful and have included it in the latter part of the survey.

This survey had its origins in late 1970, when I was enrolled in the Graduate Program in American Studies at the State University of New York in Buffalo. At the time I proposed to carry out a study of the Puerto Rican community in Buffalo. But I soon became convinced of the need for a study of more ambitious scope--one that would encompass Puerto Ricans throughout the United States. I am grateful to the Puerto Rican Legal Defense Fund and to the Metropolitan Applied Research Center (MARC) for their guidance and financial aid, which enabled me to complete this project. I also wish to acknowledge the assistance of Mary S. Strong of the MARC staff in the final editing of the text.

CONTENTS

LIST OF TABLES

ix

THE NATIONAL PROFILE: PUERTO RICANS ON THE U.S. MAINLAND

1

RAPID GROWTH OF
THE MAINLAND COMMUNITY

Puerto Rico--discovered by Columbus in 1493 and gov-
erned as a Spanish colony for four centuries--was ceded to
the United States as a result of the Spanish-American War
of 1898. The United States viewed Puerto Rico as a profit-
able site for tropical agriculture, but its main purpose
in seizing the island (given the technology of the era) was
to have a secure coaling station for its warships, thus
guaranteeing a strong U.S. naval presence in the Caribbean,
and creating a stepping stone toward the Isthmus of Panama,
where a transoceanic canal would soon be built.

Until 1917 the island was ruled as a U.S. colonial
possession, despite the clamor for more self-rule by Puerto
Ricans of all political persuasions.* It is no mere coin-
cidence that in 1917 (shortly before the United States entered into World War I) the United States purchased the
Virgin Islands from Denmark (for $25 million) and granted
American citizenship en masse to all Puerto Ricans. It
was a time when German ships prowled the Atlantic, and the
United States wished to take no chances in the Caribbean--
a key strategic zone.

Whatever the motives of the United States at the time,
however, the granting of citizenship entitled Puerto Ricans
to free access to the mainland, without passport or visa.
Before World War II, however, Puerto Rican migration to

---

*Since 1952 the island has been a commonwealth asso-
ciated with the United States. Puerto Ricans elect their
own governor and legislature. The island enjoys considerable autonomy in local affairs, but is represented by the
United States in foreign and international affairs.

the mainland was a mere trickle (see Table 1), mainly because the United States--in the midst of a great depres-
sion--offered few job opportunities to the migrant; but
also because the ocean voyage took a few days and was relatively expensive. As of 1940, only about 70,000 Puerto
Ricans lived on the mainland, and 88 percent of them were
clustered in New York City, which was the most common point
of air and sea travel between the United States and the
island.

But the situation changed radically when peace came.
An economic boom on the mainland (creating plentiful jobs
for the unskilled and semiskilled) attracted Puerto Ricans
from their homeland, where chronic unemployment remained
at high levels and where wages lagged far below mainland
standards. Furthermore, the airplane made the 1,600-mile
trip in a matter of hours, and the ticket cost little
more than a week's salary. Between 1940 and 1950, the
Puerto Rican population on the mainland more than quadru-
pled--to 301,000. This included 226,000 persons of Puerto
Rican birth and 75,000 born in the United States to Puerto
Rican parents.

Although employers in the manufacturing and service
industries welcomed the presence of a large labor pool
that would work for low wages, the general reception af-
forded the Puerto Rican migrant ranged from indifference
to outright hostility. In their 1948 book New York: Confidential, journalists Jack Lait and Lee Mortimer said:

> During the last ten years and growing every year,
> there has descended on Manhattan island like a lo-
> cust plague an influx of Puerto Ricans . . . one
> of every 13 New Yorkers is a Puerto Rican. . . .
> Puerto Ricans were not born to be New Yorkers.
> They are mostly crude farmers, subject to congen-
> ital tropical diseases, physically unfitted for
> the northern climate, unskilled, uneducated,
> non-English-speaking and almost impossible to as-
> similate and condition for healthful and useful
> existence in an active city of stone and steel.[1]

On and on they wrote, calling Puerto Ricans "poverty-
numbed, naive natives . . . alien to everything that
spells New York . . . weaklings . . . unable physically,
mentally, or financially to compete, they turn to guile
and wile and the steel blade, the traditional weapon of
the sugarcane cutter, mark of their blood and heritage."
The arrival of more Puerto Ricans, they lamented, "is
growing and the sorry end is nowhere in sight."[2]

Despite the slanderous tone of the Lait-Mortimer commentary, it is worth noting because it both articulated and helped to shape public opinion. It also demonstrated that by the late 1940s the arrival of Puerto Ricans was, indeed, having a strong impact. The most accurate part of their diatribe was their prediction that the "end" was certainly "nowhere in sight."

Between 1950 and 1960, the rate of population increase slackened, but in actual number the population grew by more than half a million to 887,000. This included 615,000 persons born in Puerto Rico and 272,000 U.S.-born Puerto Ricans. There was also a marked trend toward settling away from New York City. In 1950, nearly 82 percent of the migrants and their children resided in New York City. One decade later, this concentration was reduced to 69 percent, as communities began to grow in New Jersey, Pennsylvania, New England, and Illinois.

Between 1960 and 1970, population growth--in percentages--slackened further, but the actual increase was sizable as the community grew by more than half a million to 1.4 million.* Of this number, 783,000 persons were born in Puerto Rico, while 646,000 were born on the U.S. mainland.

Thus, for the first time, the two Puerto Rican groups (natives of the island and natives of the mainland) began to approach parity of size. And, for the first time, birth, rather than migration, became the dominant factor in the growth of the U.S. Puerto Rican community. The implications of this new balance--in cultural, economic, and political terms--are considerable.

The demographic growth rate on the island of Puerto Rico has been much slower because of the constant exodus

---

*By March 1973, the Puerto Rican population of the U.S. mainland was conservatively estimated at nearly 1.55 million. This does not include seasonal farm laborers who migrate from Puerto Rico. The Migration Division of the Puerto Rican government now supervises the contracts of 20,000; it is estimated that 30,000 to 40,000 more laborers from Puerto Rico work without formal contract. Conditions on migrant labor farms range from "excellent" to "horrible," according to a Migration Division official. In July 1974 when a New Jersey state assemblyman went to one farm in Swedesboro to check on complaints of abuses against workers, his arm was broken, allegedly in a dispute with a farm foreman.

of families to the U.S. mainland (see Table 2). Between 1960 and 1970, the island's population rose by 15.4 percent--from 2.3 million to 2.7 million. During the same period, the U.S. Puerto Rican community grew by 61.1 percent. Within that community, the number of migrants born in Puerto Rico grew by 27.3 percent, while those born on the mainland increased by a spectacular 137 percent.

THE NUMBERS CONTROVERSY

Estimates of the correct number of Puerto Ricans in the United States are a subject of controversy. The U.S. census of 1970 shows 1,429,396 persons of Puerto Rican birth or heritage on the mainland (heritage means that one's parents were born in Puerto Rico). But this figure has been challenged as far too low, and even the Census Bureau admits that there was an undercount. Jacob S. Siegel, a Census Bureau statistician, estimates that all U.S. males were undercounted by 3.3 percent and females by 1.8 percent, with variations for age and race.[3] He also estimates that black males were undercounted by 9.9 percent and black females by 5.5 percent. Blacks under age 5, he adds, were undercounted by 10.1 percent. Siegel makes no estimates for Puerto Ricans but if one uses his criteria for the total population and for blacks, Puerto Ricans would be undercounted by either 37,944 or 113,363. The deficit may be much larger, Siegel says, "We do not know whether the undercount for Puerto Ricans was higher or lower than the rate for Negroes." He adds, "It seems likely that since undercoverage rates of Negroes are higher than those of whites, the areas of large cities that have heavy concentrations of Negroes have higher undercoverage rates than areas with a more balanced racial distribution. We are . . . still concerned about the possibility that undercoverage is more serious in large cities."[4] Given that the Puerto Rican population in the United States is heavily urban (and mainly clustered in inner cities), is even poorer than the black population, and suffers from a language handicap, it does not seem illogical that the Puerto Rican undercount would be even higher than that for blacks.

To advance this theory, one can point to conflicts in school enrollment figures in New York City, where the Census Bureau overcounts black students and undercounts Puerto Ricans. The New York State Department of Education says that total 1970-71 enrollment in the city's public schools

6

(prekindergarten through 12th grade) was 1,135,298. The
Census Bureau claims that the city's public school enrollment was 1,186,542. This amounts to a Census Bureau overcount of 51,244 students, ages 3 to 34. The state report
also says there were 393,516 black students, but the census shows 418,185--an overcount of 24,669 students.

The situation reverses itself with reference to Puerto
Rican children. New York City figures on Puerto Rican
school enrollment during 1970-71 show a total of 260,040.
The Census Bureau shows an enrollment of 217,985 Puerto
Rican children, an undercount of 42,055 (or about 16 percent). The potential undercount is even greater, because
only 46.8 percent of Puerto Ricans, ages 3 to 34, are enrolled in school. If the discrepancy is also applied to
those not enrolled in school, the undercount for Puerto
Ricans, ages 3 to 34, in New York City alone is about
85,000.[5]

There are various possible reasons why the Census Bureau undercounted Puerto Ricans. Many light-skinned persons may have been counted as whites, while those of
darker skin may have been counted as blacks. Then, of
course, many may not have been counted under any category.
Another study that casts doubt upon the accuracy of the
Census Bureau count is a Population Health Survey (PHS)
carried out by the City University of New York, which estimated the city's total population in 1969-70 at 7.87 million, a figure quite close to the Census Bureau estimate
of 7.83 million.[6] Both studies has similar figures for
all boroughs, except for Manhattan, where the PHS calcu-
lated 1,683,000 compared with the Census Bureau's 1,539,000.
The discrepancy of 143,000 is "beyond the maximum antici-
pated difference due to sampling error," say the PHS au-
thors. Their survey also notes a "striking difference"
of 204,700 Puerto Ricans. That is, the Census Bureau
found 811,800 in New York City, while the PHS shows
1,016,500. (This would boost the 1970 Puerto Rican population in the United States to at least 1.6 million.)
The largest difference between the figures of the PHS and
the Census Bureau was in the 5-to-14 age group, where the
PHS found 162,000 more persons in the city--100,000 of
them being Puerto Rican.

In January 1974, the Census Bureau attempted to shed
light on the problem of the Hispanic undercount, but they
seem to have compounded the confusion. The report,[7] which
reflects the use of new criteria in measuring "persons of
Spanish origin," shows that between the time of the 1970
census and the March 1973 Current Population Survey (CPS)
there occurred the following growth:

	1970 Census	1973 CPS	
		Number	Percent Change
Total, Spanish origin	9,072,602	10,577,000	16.6
Mexican origin	4,532,435	6,293,000	38.8
Puerto Rican origin	1,429,396	1,548,000	8.3
Cuban origin	544,600	733,000	34.6
Central or South American origin	1,508,866	597,000	-60.4
Other Spanish origin	1,057,305	1,406,000	33.0

This study reveals the incredible fact that while persons of Spanish origin grew by 16.6 percent, and Mexicans and Cubans grew by more than 30 percent, Puerto Ricans grew by only 8.3 percent. Certainly there is no great difference in the birthrates among these three ethnic groups. It is strange that the Census Bureau lends credence to a report that shows the Puerto Rican population growing at a rate slower than that of other Hispanic groups. This, it appears, is an even more serious error than that which was made for the 1970 census count.

Obviously, something was wrong with the Census Bureau's methods of counting. One possible bias apparent in the March 1973 CPS questionnaire is the terminology used: in 1970, the only possible way that a person of Mexican descent could indicate his ethnic origin was to mark the circle opposite the word "Mexican"; in the March 1973 CPS, his options were expanded threefold to "Mexican American," "Chicano," and "Mexican (Mexicano)." The Census Bureau indicates that perhaps this is the reason for the dramatic increase of 38.8 percent in the Mexican origin population. If the Census Bureau were so zealous in its efforts to count the population of those of Mexican origin, one wonders why it did not use the same technique for Puerto Ricans. Both in 1970 and 1973, the only item that could be checked was "Puerto Rican." Why, one asks, were the following categories not added: "Puerto Rican-American," "Boricua," and "Neo-Rican"?

Another possible source of error is indicated by the Census Bureau itself, which stated in March 1971 that of the 8.9 million persons in the United States who reported themselves to be of Spanish origin 31.7 percent did not have a commonly known Spanish surname.[8] This fact alone could have misled some census workers in their efforts to determine ethnic origin. (A further discussion of possible reasons for an undercount is included in a later section of this book.)

Another factor that bears upon both the accuracy of the census count and the future identifiable size of the Puerto Rican community in the United States is the question of ethnic intermarriage (see Table 3). More than eight out of ten migrants born in Puerto Rico tend to marry Puerto Ricans. But among their U.S.-born children, only slightly more than half marry Puerto Ricans. If this trend continues, much of the increase due to birth may have disappeared into the "melting pot" by the next generation. The Census Bureau identifies a Puerto Rican as someone "born in Puerto Rico or born in the United States . . . with one or both parents born in Puerto Rico." Thus, according to the Census Bureau definition, the children of U.S.-born Puerto Ricans are not Puerto Rican.

These Census Bureau criteria for identifying Puerto Ricans are inconsistent and illogical, and are bound to cause controversy in future years when the children of U.S.-born Puerto Ricans become a larger numerical force. The inconsistency of the criteria is evident in the case of U.S. blacks, who are counted as blacks no matter how many generations removed they may be from their African roots. The question of Puerto Ricans is, admittedly, more complex, because they do not represent a single race. Many Puerto Ricans have Caucasian features, others are strongly Negroid, others are a mixture of the two, and some show traces of pre-Columbian Indian. If the Census Bureau definition prevails, in a couple of generations some Puerto Ricans will be lumped with U.S. blacks, others will have disappeared into the ranks of the whites, and what will happen to the mixed (and largest) group in the middle is anyone's guess. One can appreciate the Census Bureau's dilemma, but it appears that not enough thought has been given to its solution, and attempts should be made to redefine these criteria in time for the 1980 U.S. census.

OTHER HISPANIC GROUPS IN THE UNITED STATES

By 1972, nearly 9.2 million persons "of Spanish origin" lived in the United States, according to a Census Bureau survey that allows respondents to identify their own ethnic origin. This amounts to 4.5 percent of the total U.S. population (see Table 4).

In 1970, 84 percent of all Spanish-Americans lived in urban metropolitan areas, compared with 68 percent of the U.S. white population. The largest group identified was the Mexicans (5.2 million), who constituted 2.6 percent of the total U.S. population and were concentrated mainly in five Southwest states. Next in size were the Puerto Ricans (1.5 million in 1972), who constituted 0.7 percent of the nation's people. They were followed by the Cubans (629,000), the majority of whom are in Florida, and by persons of Central and South American descent (599,000) who are scattered throughout the country.

There is also a group of 1.2 million persons who—when confronted by the census takers—labeled themselves as "other Spanish"—a mysterious classification. The only possible "other Spanish" group that comes to mind is the migrant from Spain. It is most unlikely that 1.2 million Spaniards have come to the United States. It is more likely that a fair proportion of these unidentified persons are third-generation Puerto Ricans, or Puerto Ricans who for one reason or another have not properly identified themselves. In this way, many Puerto Ricans may have been miscounted, with the result that the group was undercounted. In the 1950s, when considerable publicity was given (especially in New York City) to the alleged Puerto Rican problem of slums, crime, and welfare, it is well-known that many Puerto Ricans were reluctant to identify their ethnic origin. Instead, they used the catchall label of Hispano (Hispanic). In some cases, they called themselves "Spanish," or even "Cuban."

Although there has been a surge of ethnic pride in recent years, the question is whether this pride (vociferously displayed by political militants) has filtered down to the general community. It is possible that, due to fears of racial and/or ethnic prejudice, many Puerto Ricans still prefer the comparable anonymity of being Hispanic just as many European immigrants Americanized their names and, even in physical appearance, sought to conform to their new environment. Whatever the reasons, the classification of 1.2 million people (about one of every eight persons of Spanish origin) as "other Spanish" makes them, in effect, "people without a country." Efforts should be made to seek clarification in future U.S. census surveys.

DISPERSION OF PUERTO RICANS IN
THE UNITED STATES

In 1960, Puerto Ricans lived in every state of the
union (see Table 5). The largest population by far was in
New York State (642,000). This was followed by New Jersey
(55,000), Illinois (36,000), California (28,000), Pennsylvania (21,000), Florida (19,000), Connecticut (15,000), and
Ohio (14,000). By 1970, the same states had large Puerto
Rican populations: New York (917,000), New Jersey (139,000),
Illinois (87,000), California (51,000), Pennsylvania
(44,000), Connecticut (37,000), Florida (28,000), Massachusetts (23,000), and Ohio (20,000). But the direction of
growth had shifted drastically. The New York population
grew by 42 percent. In neighboring New Jersey it grew by
150 percent; Massachusetts grew by 360 percent. Other
high growth rates were: Pennsylvania (109 percent), Illinois (141 percent), and Connecticut (146 percent).

There was also marked dispersion of Puerto Ricans to
various U.S. cities. In 1960, only ten cities had 5,000
or more Puerto Ricans. By 1970, 29 cities or urban areas
fitted that description (see Table 6). There was also
some movement away from inner cities. In Newark, for example, the bulk of the Puerto Rican population (26,000)
resided in the city in 1970. But, more than 10,000 persons lived in the urban balance around Newark, meaning
smaller towns, some almost suburban in character. Puerto
Rican residents of these fringe areas (as will be shown
later) generally have higher education levels, smaller
families, and higher incomes.

A YOUNG POPULATION

The median age for all Americans is 28 years; for
persons of Spanish origin the median is only 20.1 years;
for Puerto Ricans it is the lowest--17.9 years (see Table
7). This is even lower than the median age in Puerto
Rico, which is 21.5 years.

The probable reason for this is that large-scale Puerto
Rican migration is quite recent. As a rule, migrants were
(and are) young people of working age, with their childbearing years ahead of them. Not enough time has elapsed
for this population to mature. Also, many older Puerto
Ricans return to the island for retirement, thus steadily

lowering the median age. (More than 5 percent of all Americans are aged 65 or older, while only about 2 percent of Puerto Ricans in the United States are 65 or older.)[9]

The median age of U.S. Puerto Ricans has dropped in the past decade. In 1960 it was 21.4 years. This broke down to a median of 27.9 years for the 617,000 persons born on the island and only 5.9 years for the 275,000 U.S.-born Puerto Ricans. By 1970, the median age was 20.3 years. For migrants born in Puerto Rico it was 30.0 years, and for U.S.-born Puerto Ricans only 9.3 years. These figures suggest that two sets of demographic forces are at work: (1) the birthrate for all Puerto Ricans in the United States continues to be quite high, thus depressing median age; and (2) there seems to be some tapering off of the birthrate among U.S.-born Puerto Ricans (perhaps temporary) as their median age rises to higher levels.

These figures permit some speculation as to the nature of the Puerto Rican community in the United States in the next decade or two. First, as the U.S.-born group grows to childbearing age, there may be another population spurt of second-generation Puerto Ricans born on the mainland. Second, as the U.S.-born group ages, there will be far more U.S.-born adults earning wages, deciding where to take up residence, voting, and taking part in the civic life of their communities. The nature of their participation in these varied activities may be radically different from their island-born parents due to cultural and linguistic differences.

FAMILY SIZE

Of the 53.3 million families in the United States in 1972, about 363,000 were headed by a Puerto Rican. Each Puerto Rican family averaged 3.8 members, larger than the national average of 3.5, but fewer than the average of 4.0 persons for all families of Spanish origin (see Table 8).

Given the previous figures, it will be no surprise to learn that Puerto Rican families are young. About 55 percent of all U.S. families have children under 18; the figure for black families is 61 percent; and it is nearly 76 percent for Puerto Rican families. About 25 percent of U.S. families have children under age 6, compared with 31 percent of black families and 44 percent of Puerto Rican families. Only 1.6 percent of U.S. families have 6 or more children, compared with 5 percent of Puerto Rican families.

In 1972, about 11.6 percent of U.S. families were headed by a woman. But women headed 27.4 percent of black families and 24.1 percent of Puerto Rican families (compared with only 13.7 percent of other families of Spanish heritage). Since the breakup of a marriage almost invariably results in the woman assuming the care of the children, and since women as a group earn less than men, a high percentage of families headed by women is an economically negative factor. The presence of a single parent in the household can also result in serious problems of child care and supervision. In economic terms the average Puerto Rican family headed by a woman is at a particular disadvantage. As we shall see later in this study, Puerto Rican mothers have a very low participation rate in the labor force, and those who work earn very low wages. In New York City the figures are worse than the national average. In 1970, the Public Health Survey, previously cited, estimated that 30.9 percent of Puerto Rican families and 33.9 percent of black families were headed by a female, compared with a citywide average of 17.3 percent.

The picture improves somewhat in the case of families headed by Puerto Ricans born in the United States. They show a slightly lower percentage of women family heads, a smaller family unit, and a lower birthrate (see Table 9), all of which are factors that suggest more potential in coping with the economic pressures of urban life.

By contrast, 1970 figures for the island of Puerto Rico show that only 15.6 percent of the families were headed by women, a figure far closer to the national average. This leads one to the tempting hypothesis that conditions in Puerto Rico are more hospitable to family stability; that the trauma of migration to a new, somewhat hostile environment disrupts family stability; and that there is a slight recovery in the next generation born in the United States. However, there are insufficient data at hand to prove this hypothesis. To do so, one would require data on family stability, not for all of Puerto Rico, but for those families that migrate, to see how closely they conform to islandwide figures. These data are not available.

Further complicating the picture is the fact that family stability (as measured by percentage of women family heads) has declined considerably since 1960 (see Table 9), when only 13.6 percent of Puerto Rican families in the United States were headed by a woman. Again, it is tempting to describe this as an erosion of family stability brought on by the social pressures of migration, but data are lacking.

13

FUTURE GROWTH

For many reasons the future growth of the U.S. Puerto Rican community is difficult, if not impossible, to chart. The bulk of growth has taken place in the past three decades. Departures and arrivals at San Juan's airport soared from 49,000 in 1940 to 4.2 million in 1969 (see Table 10). While many of these back-and-forth trips were made by North American tourists on Caribbean holidays, most travelers were Puerto Ricans who came to visit friends and relatives or to reside for varying lengths of time. Despite the nearly thousandfold increase in airport movement, the net outflow from Puerto Rico has decreased, probably due to a combination of improved job opportunities on the island and a shrinkage of available employment in the United States. Between 1950 and 1959, the average yearly outflow from Puerto Rico was 46,000 persons. The next decade, from 1960 to 1969, was a period of record economic growth in Puerto Rico and the annual outflow averaged only 14,000 persons.

The picture for the 1970s is still hazy, but there seems to be an upward trend in migration, caused by troubled economic conditions on the island. For the past decade or more, Puerto Rico has had a phenomenal growth rate of about 10 percent yearly, but during the first nine months of fiscal 1973, the island suffered a negative economic growth of minus 2.9 percent.[10] However, the United States has been plagued by its own problems of economic stagnation, and jobs are not as abundant as they were in the 1960s.

Perhaps for these reasons the following unofficial figures for net migration from Puerto Rico in the 1970s reflect a trend that is lower than the 1950s, but higher than the 1960s:[11]

1970	20,715
1971	4,951
1972	34,015
1973	20,948

Since Puerto Ricans are American citizens, and have unlimited access to the mainland, it is hard to predict whether the migration flow will increase, hold steady or virtually dry up. As in the past, economic opportunities (or the lack of them) will almost certainly be the deciding factor. However, if the U.S. Puerto Rican population increases by 61 percent in the present decade (as it did in the previous one), it will reach at least 2.3 million by 1980, a figure not far below the island's 1970 population. It is not inconceivable that at some point in the future, perhaps in the late 1980s, Puerto Ricans in the diaspora will outnumber their compatriots on the island.

The birthrate is, of course, another factor. Because so many Puerto Ricans migrated to the United States with their childbearing years ahead of then, the mainland community is more prolific than the population in Puerto Rico. For example, the fertility rate for Puerto Ricans in the United States is 509, compared with 481 in Puerto Rico.*

In the United States, the Puerto Rican birthrate is higher than that of the general population, but U.S.-born Puerto Rican women not only have fewer children than migrant women born on the island, but in the upper-age brackets (25-44 years old) have fewer children than the average American woman (see Table 11). Since Puerto Rican populations are centered in urban areas, where rents are high and living space is at a premium, the pressures to reduce family size are enormous. The trend, then, seems to be one of considerable population growth in the next few years with a gradual tapering off of the rate of growth as U.S.-born Puerto Rican women become a larger factor.

Coupled with this growth, however, there remains the question of cultural and ethnic assimilation. At present, the Census Bureau counts as Puerto Rican only those persons born on the island, or those whose parents were born on the island. One can speculate on whether or not third- and fourth-generation Puerto Ricans in the United States will identify with their ethnic group or will disappear into the so-called melting pot. The complex play of cultural, racial, economic, and political forces in the coming decade will bear heavily upon the outcome.

Since the Puerto Rican migration coincided almost exactly with the growth of jet travel, Puerto Ricans can practically commute back and forth to their homeland. Thus, in the foreseeable future, the U.S. Puerto Rican community offers a spectrum of varying degrees of ethnicity: the never-ending flux of new arrivals from the island; the

---

*The fertility rate is based on children under age 5 per 1,000 women, 15-49 years old. Figures for Puerto Ricans in the United States, from 1970 Census Report PC(2)-1E, Table 2, p. 8; for Puerto Ricans on the island, from 1970 Census Report PC(1)-B53, Table 14, pp. 53-47.

established mainland residents, born in Puerto Rico, who
came to the United States at times ranging from infancy to
middle age; those born in the United States, a fair number
of whom marry members of other ethnic groups; and from
among all these types many thousands of persons who travel
back and forth each year or every few years and never es-
tablish a wholly permanent residence either in the United
States or on the island. It is a community of great com-
plexity and constant change.

The Puerto Rican population on the island is not
static either. In 1960, 2.1 percent of the population con-
sisted of U.S.-born Puerto Ricans, and 2.8 percent represented persons who had resided on the mainland five years
previous to the census. By 1970, U.S.-born Puerto Ricans
who had returned to the island constituted 4 percent of
the population, and 5.4 percent of the population had
lived in the United States five years prior to the census
(see Table 12). Thus, there was already some back-flow to
Puerto Rico, while other Puerto Ricans were migrating to
the United States. By 1970, Puerto Rico's public schools
were already setting up special bilingual programs to deal
with at least 11,000 children who had come from the mainland and could speak little Spanish.

NOTES

1. Jack Lait and Lee Mortimer, New York: Confidential
(Chicago: Ziff-Davis, 1948), p. 126.
2. Ibid., p. 128.
3. Jacob S. Siegel, U.S. Bureau of the Census, "Estimates of Coverage of the Population by Sex, Race, and
Age in the 1970 Census," 36 pp. Paper presented at the
annual meeting of the Population Association of America,
New Orleans, La., April 26, 1973, p. 24.
4. Ibid.
5. Calculations based on comparing the following doc-
uments: U.S. Census Bureau, "1970 Census of Population,
General Social and Economic Characteristics of New York,"
PC (1)-634-NY and the University of the State of New York,
Information Center on Education, Albany, N.Y., "1970-71
Annual Education Summary. Statistical and Financial Summary of Education in New York State for the Year Ending
June 30, 1971," 203 pp.
6. Morey J. Wantman, et al., "Estimates of Population Characteristics, New York City, 1964-65-66-68-70,"
Population Health Survey Research Bulletin RB-P14-72.

Center for Social Research, City University of New York, December 1972, 40 pp.

7. U.S. Bureau of the Census, "Population Characteristics, Persons of Spanish Origin in the United States: March, 1973," Series P-20, No. 259, January 1974, 4 pp.

8. U.S. Census Bureau, "Persons of Spanish Origin in the United States, March 1971 and 1972," Series P-20, No. 250, April 1973, p. 6.

9. 1970 Census Report, "United States Summary," PC (1)-C1, Table 85, pp. 1-380; and 1970 Census Report, "Puerto Ricans in the United States," PC (2)-1E, Table 2, p. 4.

10. San Juan Star, May 19, 1974, p. 1. In terms of straight monetary growth, the island showed a 7.7 percent increase, but this was canceled out by a 10.9 percent inflation rate.

11. Secured in a telephone conversation with an official of the Office of the Commonwealth of Puerto Rico in New York City. The figures, he said, reflect the difference between arrivals and departures at San Juan International Airport and were supplied to him by the Commonwealth Department of Labor in San Juan.

2

**EDUCATION,
LANGUAGE, AND
LITERACY**

For the most part, mainland Puerto Ricans have less
formal education than whites, blacks, or other Hispanic
groups (see Tables 13 and 14). The average number (8.6)
of school years completed by Puerto Ricans today is nearly
the same as it was for the U.S. population 30 years ago.
Nearly 24 percent of Puerto Rican adults (ages 25 and
above) have completed less than 5 years of school, compared
with 5 percent of the total U.S. population and 13.5 percent of the black population. Only 19.8 percent of Puerto
Rican adults have completed 4 years of high school, compared with a U.S. average of 56.4 percent and 34.7 percent
for blacks. (In the 35-54 age bracket, when most men and
women are at the peak of their earning capacity, only 6
percent of Americans showed less than 5 years of schooling,
compared with 60 percent for Puerto Ricans.)

AGE AND EDUCATION

There is some improvement in the amount of education
attained by younger Puerto Ricans. For example, among
those ages 25 to 29, only 1 in 16 has not completed 5
years of school. Still, this is far behind the U.S. average of 1 in 120. According to a 1969 census survey,
Puerto Ricans 35 years and older had 7.5 median school
years, while those in the 25-to-34 age bracket had completed 9.9 median school years. There were also higher
levels of high school and college graduation for the
younger group (see Table 15).
Part of this situation is, in a sense, imported from
Puerto Rico, since migrants come to the United States with

a low level of schooling. In Puerto Rico in 1970, nearly 38 percent of all adults (aged 25 or more) had less than 5 years of schooling, a record twice as poor as that of Puerto Ricans in the United States (see Table 16). In Puerto Rico, on the other hand, 27 percent of all adults had completed at least four years of high school, slightly better than the achievement of mainland Puerto Rican adults.

The level of school years completed among U.S. Puerto Ricans (8.6 years) is clearly higher than the figure on the island (6.9 years). But, again, in the area of higher education, figures on the island are better: 6 percent of all adults in Puerto Rico are college graduates, compared with 2.2 percent of U.S. Puerto Ricans (refer again to Table 16).

These figures suggest that class lines in Puerto Rico may be more rigid than on the mainland. In Puerto Rico, students from the long-established middle and upper classes account for relatively high percentages of high school and college graduates. At the same time, there are large masses of people with virtually no education at all (indicated by the 6.9 figure). The mainland population consists almost entirely of migrants who emerged from that uneducated class. Those who have graduated from high school or college are still relatively few in number (contrasted with the 52 percent of all Americans who are high school graduates and 10 percent who have college degrees). The higher level of median school years for mainland Puerto Ricans suggests a more egalitarian, albeit painfully slow, advance in education.* But even this fact does not permit any sweeping conclusions. For example, figures since 1950 show ever-rising levels of education for Puerto Rican migrants and their children in the United States. However, the rate of improvement in median school years has been more rapid in Puerto Rico (see Table 17).

SCHOOL ENROLLMENT

There has been some improvement in school enrollment among U.S. Puerto Ricans (see Table 18); the figures compare favorably with enrollment of students in Puerto Rico (see Table 19). By 1970, 72 percent of U.S. Puerto Rican

*It could also suggest that many Puerto Rican and other minority children are passed from grade to grade, but are given little education.

children, ages 5 to 6 were enrolled in school as compared
with 66 percent in 1960. In the older age groups (25 to
34) a clear dichotomy emerges between migrants from Puerto
Rico and U.S.-born children. This is the age bracket
where a student would be engaged in college work or some
form of technical-vocational training. For the entire
U.S. Puerto Rican community, ages 25 to 34, the enrollment
figure is 2.5 percent. But it is 1.9 percent for migrants
and 6.8 percent for U.S.-born children. This latter figure virtually matches the nationwide average of 6.9 percent for urban metropolitan areas. This is just one of
several indications that U.S.-born Puerto Ricans achieve
higher levels of education than their migrant parents.
In 1960, for example, the migrants had 8.0 median school
years completed, while their children had 10.8 median
school years. By 1970, migrants had risen to 8.4 median
school years, while at the same time U.S.-born children
had achieved a median of 11.5 school years, which was between the figure for all Americans (12.1 years) and the
figure for "Negro and Other Races" (10.0 years). These
are promising signs, but it should be remembered that fully
half of the U.S.-born Puerto Ricans are under the age of
9, and the adult migrant, born in Puerto Rico, is far more
representative of the community.

DROPOUTS

     Dropping out of school is still a severe problem for
both groups of Puerto Ricans, although the figures are
better for U.S.-born students (see Table 20). In 1970
among all Puerto Ricans in the United States, ages 16 to
21, 55 percent were not in school and 36 percent of these
dropouts were without jobs. Among the U.S.-born, the dropout rate was lower, 39 percent,but those out of school
were unemployed at the rate of 43 percent.
     In the 16-to-21 age bracket the dropout rate for all
Americans in the Northeast was 32 percent, and unemployment of dropouts was much lower, about 16 percent. In
fact, while Puerto Ricans represented only about 3 percent
of the males, ages 16 to 21, in the northeastern United
States they constituted 5 percent of the school dropouts,
and more than 12 percent of the unemployed.
     New York City gives us the largest sample of Puerto
Rican students; their achievement figures may be on the
pessimistic side since they do not include children from
upwardly mobile Puerto Rican families that constantly move

from the city. There has been a marked change in the
ethnic composition of the city's schools. In 1960, about
37 percent of the students were black or Puerto Rican; by
1970, this group made up 57 percent of school enrollment.

In 1970, although 25 percent of the city's elementary
schoolchildren were Puerto Rican, only 15 percent of the
students in the academic high schools were Puerto Rican.
This indicates a high dropout rate or a diversion to vocational schools where Puerto Ricans have 28 percent of the
enrollment. These figures assure an underrepresentation
of Puerto Ricans in college in future years and ultimately
in the professions. On the other hand, between 1960 and
1970, there was a marked increase in both the size and
ratio of Puerto Rican enrollment in academic high schools.
While the elementary school population of Puerto Ricans
rose by about 45 percent, academic high school enrollment
rose by 240 percent. However, one must be cautious in
trying to measure qualitative change by mere numbers.
In the same way that today's increased dollars do not al-
ways equate to equivalent buying power, one must ask
whether the quality of the city's academic high schools
is the same as it was in 1960. There are many allegations
that as ethnic minorities become dominant in a school, the
quality of education is reduced. Whether this is true,
to what degree, and why, are hard to quantify. The key
question is whether such an alleged drop in quality is
caused by the students or is due to the inability of the
school system to respond adequately to shifting cultural
and economic situations.

The mere passage of time is no guarantee of improvement and progress, as reflected in the following data from
New York City. Between 1960 and 1970, the percentage of
white college graduates residing in the city jumped from
9 percent to 13 percent. Among blacks, the figure remained
at 4 percent during the decade. In 1970, only 1 percent
of the city's Puerto Ricans had a college degree, a very
slight gain over 1960.

TEACHER SHORTAGE

There are confusing, often contradictory, reports as
to the progress of minority group students. In late 1973,
a New York City school official said that tests given the
previous spring "show that citywide averages are better
than those of 1972 in 11 grades, except grade 8, where
they are the same." A New York State official opined "we

may have turned the corner in reading and math," but cautioned that the city continues to have "an above-average percentage of low-scoring pupils" in reading and math. The state tested students and found steady gains over three consecutive years. The city tested students and found a decline.[1]

The question "can Johnny read?" might also be accompanied, in poorer school districts, by "can Johnny see?" It is alarming to learn that--in the most advanced nation on earth--a study of visual problems among East Harlem students found that 30 percent of the Puerto Rican children were myopic (nearsighted) and fewer than a quarter of these children wore adequately prescribed glasses. The study revealed two to three times more myopia among the Puerto Rican children than among the blacks or whites tested. Of the Puerto Ricans aged 11 and older, 56 percent of the girls and 45 percent of the boys were nearsighted and required glasses. Of those who had glasses, 70 percent had inadequate lenses.[2]

Perhaps the most distressing fact of all in the area of education is the drastic shortage of Puerto Rican teachers in the New York public schools. This results in a linguistic and cultural barrier between students and teachers. All minorities are underrepresented in the teaching profession. The 1970 census showed that 89,473 teachers resided in New York City. Black student enrollment accounts for 34 percent of the children, but the city had only 7,358 black teachers--about 8.2 percent of the total. The situation is far worse for Puerto Ricans who constitute 22.8 percent of the city's classroom enrollment. The city had only 978 Puerto Rican teachers--only 1.1 percent of the teaching staff. If the ratio were corrected, the city school system alone would require 20,000 more Puerto Rican teachers. One shrinks from the thought of establishing rigid quota systems, whereby the percentage of Puerto Rican students would be matched by a similar ratio of Puerto Rican teachers, but the present situation is clearly inequitable and cries out for change. Pressure for change, however, will certainly be met with stiff resistance from teachers' unions, which have lamentably shown that they are sometimes more concerned with bureaucratic survival than with the resolution of urgent pedagogical needs.

MOTHER TONGUE

Of the total U.S. population in late 1969, 81.6 percent reported English as their mother tongue and 3.4 percent reported Spanish. Among Puerto Ricans in the United States, only 16 percent reported English as their mother tongue (see Table 21). In the same survey, about three out of every four Puerto Ricans said that Spanish was the language usually spoken in the home (see Table 22).

Age and gender as well as ethnicity are also factors that appear to determine one's ability to read and write English. In 1969 more than 80 percent of U.S. Puerto Ricans, ages 10 to 24, reported that they could read and write English. However, for those aged 25 or older, only 60 percent had that capability. Among U.S. Puerto Rican men, the figure was 73 percent, but only 66 percent for women. The language gap between men and women is less pronounced at younger ages (see Table 23).

Because Spanish is the mother tongue of most Puerto Ricans in the United States, its usage has increased greatly in the communities where migrants reside, particularly in the New York-New Jersey metropolitan area. There are Spanish-language newspapers, magazines, and radio and television programs. Many stores have Spanish-speaking personnel. Government institutions have displayed less alacrity in responding to this need.

BILINGUAL FACILITIES

In late 1973 a federal district court judge in New York City ordered the Board of Elections to run a bilingual election on November 6, 1973, with all amendments, propositions. and voting instructions printed in Spanish as well as English. The board was also directed to assign translators to all polling places in areas where the 1970 census showed 5 percent or more Spanish-speaking residents.[3] This order was not the result of government initiative, but was brought about as a result of a suit filed by the Puerto Rican Legal Defense and Education Fund and Bronx Democrat City Councilman Ramón S. Velez. They claimed that the conduct of an election solely in English violates several federal voting rights laws. It was estimated that

about half of the city's 1,599 polling places would require translators. A key point made by the plaintiffs
was that in Puerto Rico--where elections are conducted in
Spanish--voter participation is higher than in most states,
whereas Puerto Rican migrants to the mainland have a very
low level of voter participation.

Even this small victory for the use of Spanish in
New York City elections was diminished when the system was
first put into effect. During the primary elections held
in September 1974, the Spanish translation on the primary
ballot was "so full of mistakes that Spanish-speaking
voters may be confused or seriously misled by badly trans-
lated voting instructions that, in one case, say exactly
the opposite of the English original."[4] With more than
1 million Puerto Ricans in New York, the Board of Elections
chose a non-Puerto Rican (the author of a Spanish-language
column for a union newspaper) to translate the ballot text.
Indicative of the widespread ignorance of and insensitivity
to the problem was the comment later by Board of Elections
executive director James Siket: "If he can write Puerto
Rican for a newspaper, I felt he was good."[5] Despite this
setback, the principle of bilingualism has been established
and is also slowly being recognized in the states of New
Jersey and Massachusetts, which have large Puerto Rican
populations.

The language crisis for Spanish-speaking people is
greatest in the schools. In New York City, for example,
about 100,000 of the Hispanic students have a poor command
of English, and some 86 percent are below normal in reading levels for their grade and age; more than 57 percent
of the Hispanic students drop out of school, compared with
46 percent of blacks and 29 percent of whites. The language barrier may not be the only problem; but it is certain that little education can take place if the teachers
are unable to communicate with their students. The city
has 22 bilingual programs, but these reach only 4,000
children, leaving more than 100,000 Hispanic children without proper help.[6]

"It is no wonder that Puerto Rican children are scor-
ing poorly on standardized tests, dropping out of school
at an extraordinary rate (52 percent between 10th and 12th
grades), failing to take advantage of post-secondary
school opportunities, and finding it very difficult to
compete in the job market," said the Fleischmann Commission, which has studied the problem. Organizations representing the Puerto Rican community have also taken the issue of bilingual education to court in order to secure

more emphasis on Spanish-language studies. This would allow students to learn the curriculum while they also improve their English.

Thus far no real breakthrough has been made, despite
a Board of Education study in New York that urges a change
in present conditions, "which are contributing to the
failure of Puerto Rican children in the classroom."[7] The
study stated that the city had only 800 bilingual classroom teachers, and that a fivefold increase--to 4,200--
was needed if the 105,000 pupils with difficulty in English
were to be organized into classes of 25 for help. Again,
the powerful teaching union in New York City has demonstrated more concern with its own survival, and with main-
taining the status quo, rather than addressing itself to
this urgent pedagogical crisis.

NOTES

1. New York _Times_, September 20, 1973, p. 65.
2. Ibid., June 26, 1973, p. 14.
3. Ibid., September 28, 1973, p. 1.
4. Ibid., September 10, 1974, p. 82.
5. Ibid.
6. San Juan _Star_, August 7, 1972, p. 32. (An AP
report from Washington, D.C.)
7. Ibid., May 8, 1972, p. 34.

3

In recent years, senior economic advisers to the federal government have maintained that a goal of reducing unemployment in the United States to 4 percent (it was below 4 percent in 1966) ought to be abandoned and a 5 percent target substituted on the grounds that attempts to achieve a 4 percent goal would create "more inflation, shortages in certain skilled jobs, and the risk of a severe recession in the long run." Adopting a 5 percent unemployment goal for the nation amounts to virtually condemning Puerto Ricans and other minorities to figures at least double that. Nationwide,the nonwhite jobless ratio in comparison to the white has been 1.8 to 1, with nonwhite unemployment being 8.2 percent when unemployment for whites was 4.5 percent.[1] By 1974, unemployment among whites was roughly 5 percent, meaning a jobless rate of 9 percent for nonwhites.

LABOR FORCE PARTICIPATION

Puerto Ricans appear to be the hardest hit of all in a shrinking job market. To begin with, they have a relatively low rate of participation in the U.S. labor force (see Table 24). In 1972, about 295,000 Puerto Rican men were in the U.S. labor force, representing about 76 percent of the Puerto Rican men of working age. Among all American men, 86 percent were in the labor force.

The difference is even more striking among women. The 108,000 Puerto Rican women in the labor force represented only 26 percent of Puerto Rican women of working age (16-64). The labor force participation rate among all

U.S. women is nearly 50 percent, about double that of Puerto
Rican women.

The inference to be drawn is obvious. With fewer persons of working age in the labor force, less income is de-
rived. The reasons for this low participation rate need
be explored in greater detail.* Also, there are some con-
flicting data, which will be discussed later in this survey. Figures do show--for some age groups--a somewhat
higher labor force participation among Puerto Ricans born
in the United States, compared with migrants; but this
group makes a relatively small impact upon the total picture (see Table 25).

The low involvement of women in the labor force has
had a crippling effect upon the income of the Puerto Rican
family. Certainly there are complex reasons for this situation. The need to care for young children is one, but
even here Puerto Rican women with young children rank low
in comparison with mothers from other racial or ethnic
groups. Among women with children under the age of six,
28 percent of whites and 47 percent of blacks are in the
labor force. The figure for Puerto Ricans is only 16 percent. Only where women have no children under age 18 is
there some parity: 41 percent for whites, 43 percent for
blacks, and 40 percent for Puerto Ricans (see Table 26).
One suspects that more day care facilities in Hispanic
neighborhoods might have a favorable impact in freeing
mothers for work, but even this is a futile exercise if
jobs are not available.

UNEMPLOYMENT

According to March 1972 figures, Puerto Ricans have
the highest unemployment rate of virtually all ethnic or
racial groups in the United States (see Table 27). While
6 percent of all U.S. men were jobless, the figure was
7.4 percent for men of Spanish origin, and 8.8 percent for
Puerto Rican men. Among women, unemployment was 6.6 percent nationwide, 10 percent for women of Spanish origin,
and 17.6 percent for Puerto Rican women.

These figures do not describe the true picture. It
is worse. The rate of unemployment refers to that portion

---

*A similar low labor force participation rate prevails
in Puerto Rico. In 1970, it was 54.7 percent for men and
22.9 percent for women (ages 14 to 64).

of the civilian labor force that is jobless. However, the "civilian labor force" is not synonymous with the entire working-age population. It includes only those persons who are working or actively seeking work. It does not include disabled persons. It does not include persons who, for various reasons (lack of skills, lack of opportunity in geographic area, and so forth) are not actively seeking work. In other words, the chronically unemployed, those who have lost hope, are not included in official unemployment statistics.

For example, 86 percent of all Americans, ages 16 to 64, are in the labor force. Among Puerto Ricans, the figure drops to 76.6 percent. If Puerto Ricans participated in the labor force at the same level as the total population and the number of persons with jobs remained constant, unemployment among Puerto Rican men would be more accurately depicted--not at the "official" rate of 8.8 percent-- but at the "adjusted" (and more realistic) level of 18.7 percent. Among Puerto Rican women, the "official" rate of 17.6 percent "adjusts" upward to 56.4 percent. For both men and women, the "official" rate of 12.6 percent soars to 33.0 percent.* In other words, about one of every three working age Puerto Ricans in the United States is without a job (see Table 28).

Such a high level of unemployment represents a disaster of serious proportions. Amid the affluence of the United States, Puerto Ricans are living in conditions worse than those of the Great Depression of the 1930s. And time has not improved the situation. In 1960, the labor force participation rate for Puerto Rican men and women was better than it is today. At that time (1960), 79 percent of Puerto Rican men, aged 14 and older, were in the labor force as were 36 percent of the women. Since most other indexes, such as education and literacy, showed some improvement between 1960 and 1970, it appears that the job market in 1960 may have been more favorable for the skills offered by Puerto Rican workers. Other reasons may also be cited for the low labor force participation rate. Health is one. About 25 percent of all Puerto Rican men under age 65 and outside the labor force were listed as "disabled" in 1971.[2] Only 25 percent of white U.S. women

---

*This, incidentally, is about the same situation as in Puerto Rico, where the real rate is far higher than the official rate, which has been between 10 and 12 percent for many years.

had to care for children under age 6, compared with 44
percent of Puerto Rican women.

There is a far different picture of labor force participation among husband-wife families. In fact, Puerto
Rican husbands ranked very high in comparison with other
ethnic groups. In 1970, in a comparison of those husbands
who "worked at some time during the year," the Census Bureau found that Puerto Rican husbands had a labor force
participation rate of 88.9 percent, compared with 89.9
percent for all white husbands and 88.8 percent for blacks.
In the category of husbands who "worked full time year
round," Puerto Ricans ranked highest of all--with 71.1
percent--compared with 69.3 percent for whites and 62.2
percent for blacks.[3]

TYPES OF OCCUPATION

In 1970, only 4 percent of Puerto Ricans in New York,
New Jersey, and Pennsylvania held "professional or technical jobs, compared with 15 percent for whites and 5.8 percent for blacks. Puerto Ricans had 4.2 percent of the
jobs as managers and administrators, compared with 12 percent for whites and 3 percent for blacks. Puerto Ricans
were behind whites, but not blacks, in sales jobs; they
were behind whites, and about even with blacks, in jobs as
craftsmen. The largest single occupation for Puerto Ricans
in the three Middle Atlantic states was operatives, meaning
factory workers, where they showed 25 percent. About 13
percent of the whites and 19 percent of the blacks were in
that category (see Table 29).

One hears of small gains in job status, some of them
symbolic. In October 1973, Siglinda Sanchez of Hoboken,
New Jersey became the first Puerto Rican to work as a page
in the U.S. House of Representatives. In August 1971,
Mario Hernandez became the first high school principal of
Puerto Rican extraction in New York City's history (at the
same time, about one of every five students in the city
was Hispanic). One also hears of "recruitment drives" in
local, state, and federal agencies to bring more minority
members into jobs. But how much remains to be done can be
illustrated in New York City, where Hispanics make up
about 15 percent of the population, but only about 1.7 percent of the city's 30,000-man police force. New York
State's government has demonstrated some improvement in
hiring practices. In 1969, for example, Puerto Ricans constituted 1.6 percent of state employees. By the next year,

this figure increased to 1.8 percent and 4.7 percent of
new employees hired were Puerto Rican. However, most jobs
were at the lowest levels. About 81 percent of Puerto
Ricans employed by the state earned below $8,922 a year
in 1970, compared with 78 percent of blacks and 44 percent
of whites. Of those earning $13,000 or more per year, the
figure was 23 percent of whites, 6 percent of blacks, and
7.7 percent of the Puerto Ricans.[4]

LOW INCOME AND FALLING BEHIND

The Puerto Rican family has the lowest income of any
major racial or ethnic group in the United States and it
is not catching up. In 1971, median family income for
Puerto Ricans was $6,185, compared with $10,672 for whites,
$6,440 for blacks, and $7,548 for all families of Spanish
origin.*

Furthermore, 29 percent of Puerto Rican families were
below the "low income" threshold, compared with 8.6 percent
of whites and 29.8 percent of blacks (see Table 30). While
only one of every 12 American families earned less than
$3,000 per year, this was the case for one of every six
Puerto Rican families. On the other hand, nearly four of
every ten American families earned $12,000 or more per
year, while only one Puerto Rican family in ten reached
that level (see Table 31).

Even among the experienced labor force, Puerto Ricans
have been unable to gain access to higher-paying jobs.
In the three Middle Atlantic states, Puerto Rican male pro-
fessionals and managers had median earnings of only $7,441,
compared with $11,874 for whites. The same held true for
factory workers (operatives): Puerto Ricans had median
earnings of $5,239, compared with $7,220 for whites.

---

*Among families of Spanish origin are those that belong
to the mysterious "other Spanish" category, many of them
may be Puerto Ricans. Since this group has a significantly
higher income, it would be advantageous for the U.S. Census
Bureau to identify the Puerto Rican families in the group.
For one thing, it would offer useful data on how well, or
badly, the American Dream is working (the concept that
America is a land of opportunity for all). If a substantial number of Puerto Rican families move up the economic
ladder and are no longer identified as Puerto Rican, it is
impossible to gauge the extent of upward social mobility
of the entire group.

The degree to which this situation may be caused by racial and/or ethnic prejudice is difficult to document, but that prejudice exists is without question. Certainly levels of education and ability to communicate in English are also crucial factors. For example, Puerto Ricans with four or more years of high school earn $1,000 more per year than those with an eighth grade education. But it is also valid to ask: should not the differential be even greater for those with a high school diploma (see Table 32)? There is also a clear difference in earnings between Puerto Rican workers whose mother tongue is English and those whose dominant language is Spanish. For example, 17 percent of the Spanish-speakers earn below $3,000 per year, while this is the case for only 7.7 percent of the English-speakers. Also, nearly 35 percent of English-speakers earn $10,000 or more, compared with fewer than 8 percent of Spanish-speakers (see Table 33).

Again, as to family income, we see evidence of the growing dichotomy between Puerto Rican migrants and U.S.-born Puerto Ricans. In 1970, median income for all Puerto Rican families in the United States was $6,924. For families headed by a person born in Puerto Rico, the median income was $5,987. Family heads born in the United States had a median income of $7,435--a difference of $28 per week. By the same token, while nearly 28 percent of families headed by Puerto Rican migrants were below the poverty level, the figure was 20 percent for U.S.-born family heads. This is some improvement, but still nearly double the figure for all American families below the poverty level (10.7 percent).

Income has increased substantially for Puerto Ricans in the United States since 1959, but at a slower rate than it has for white and black families. In relative terms, Puerto Rican families earn less than they did in 1959, before the declaration of the so-called War on Poverty. At that time Puerto Rican family income was 65 percent of white family income and blacks earned 54 percent of white family income. By 1971 black families had climbed to 60 percent of white family income, and Puerto Ricans earned less than 58 percent of whites--they had fallen behind blacks and fallen farther behind whites (see Table 34).*

---

*Both black and Puerto Rican family income declined in relation to white families by 1971. See Table 34. On August 8, 1974, the New York Times reported that real purchasing power for persons of Spanish origin was unchanged from 1969 to 1973, while it increased 4 percent for the entire U.S. population.

The economic recession in the United States that began in 1969 has had a severe impact upon Puerto Ricans who, like members of other minorities, are "last hired, first fired." In 1969, 10.7 percent of persons in the United States fell below the low-income level. By 1970, the poor had increased to 12.6 percent and stayed at 12.5 percent in 1971. Among Puerto Ricans, the low-income group increased during those three years from 29 percent to 29.2 percent to 32.2 percent (see Table 35). Statistics sound dry in comparison with the fact that 73,000 more Puerto Ricans dipped below the poverty level in that period. These figures should also be compared with Washington statements that the federal government has redoubled its efforts to help Hispanic peoples.

HOUSING AND INCOME

Housing is inextricably linked with income in several ways. Where a person lives determines to a great extent the options available to him or her on the job market. Whether a person is a homeowner also affects income--in terms of building up equity in real estate--especially in this era of inflation and rising rental costs. Only 14.8 percent of U.S. Puerto Rican families own the dwellings in which they reside, compared with 59.1 percent of American families (the figure is slightly higher--22.4 percent-- for families headed by a U.S.-born Puerto Rican). The median value of owner-occupied dwellings is lower for Puerto Ricans than it is for all American urban families. Also, nearly two out of three Puerto Rican families do not own an automobile, which limits their mobility in seeking jobs far from home (see Table 36).

Because Puerto Ricans are predominantly urban and poor, they are often forced to live in multifamily dwellings that tend to deteriorate the quality of life. For example, a three-year study by New York University indicates that the nature of housing can be a determining factor in the crime rate, even when other factors such as racial or ethnic composition and income are relatively constant. NYU's Institute of Planning and Housing made an analysis of 1969 crime statistics compiled by the New York City Housing Authority for 100 low-income public housing projects. It showed that in three-floor walk-up buildings, there were 30 serious crimes per 1,000 families; in buildings of six or seven floors, there were 41 serious crimes per 1,000 families; and in high-rise structures, from 13 to 30 floors, there were 68 serious crimes per 1,000 families. Thus they found that "the higher the building . . . the higher the crime rate," and that crime in high-rise elevator dwellings was more than double the rate in smaller, walk-up structures.[5] High-rise public housing projects were planned and built--not by the poor--by municipal, state, and federal planners who, in their zeal to achieve high density and lower cost per unit, apparently created conditions that are conducive to antisocial behavior.

POVERTY AND WELFARE

In 1970, 24 percent of all Puerto Rican families in the United States relied on some form of public assistance to provide--or supplement--income. This amounted to 18 percent for families headed by a U.S.-born Puerto Rican, which was still far higher than the percentage of all American families that receive some welfare aid. Again, however, one must remember that the "U.S.-born" factor is still small: in 1970, there were only 40,590 U.S.-born family heads, compared with 288,276 family heads that were born in Puerto Rico (see Table 37).

New York City contains by far the largest number of Puerto Ricans living in poverty, and the number of welfare recipients has risen dramatically: from 332,000 in 1959 to 1.2 million in January 1972. However, other areas of the United States have risen even faster in welfare payments. Between 1964 and 1971, New York was tenth among selected major urban centers, behind areas in Texas, Michigan, Oregon, Ohio, Massachusetts, and Pennsylvania. The city was fifth among major urban centers in terms of recipients of aid to dependent children in proportion to its population (11.1 percent). It was behind Newark (12.6 percent), Baltimore (12.5 percent), Boston (12.0 percent), and Philadelphia (11.3 percent). Other high-ranking areas were Atlanta, San Francisco, Los Angeles, St. Louis, and the District of Columbia.

Of New York City's welfare recipients, the U.S. Labor Department showed in December of 1971 that only 2.6 percent were employable; of the remainder, 2.5 percent were employed persons receiving income supplements; 6.2 percent were aged adults over 65; 11.9 percent were disabled adults; 20 percent were adults caring for children; and 56.8 percent were children under age 21.

When New York City attempted to screen welfare mothers in late 1973, 65 percent of the 10,000 women examined were

found to have severe disabilities. The city estimated
that about 60,000 of the 250,000 mothers receiving welfare
would legitimately meet the "disabled" standard, meaning
that, even if child care facilities were available, they
were too physically handicapped to work and support their
families.[6]

NOTES

1. New York _Times_, May 20, 1971, p. 37.
2. _Monthly Labor Review_, April 1973, p. 5.
3. Ibid., p. 8.
4. Buffalo _Evening News_, July 28, 1971, p. 18.
5. New York _Times_, October 26, 1972, p. 45.
6. Ibid., February 2, 1974, p. 10; excerpts from the
President's Annual Economic Report of 1974.

II

STATE AND
CITY PROFILES:
PUERTO RICANS IN
U.S. URBAN AREAS

AN OVERVIEW OF POPULATION
CONCENTRATIONS

Although 1.5 million Puerto Ricans on the mainland
are scattered through every state in the union, at least
two-thirds of them reside in the three Middle Atlantic
states of New York, New Jersey, and Pennsylvania. It is
for these three states that one can find a relative abun-
dance of Census Bureau data on the state, county, and city
levels that compare the socioeconomic status of Puerto
Ricans with that of white and black residents of the same
area.*

Elsewhere in the United States, with few exceptions,
Puerto Ricans are such small minority components of the
general population that they are not given special attention in the census as a separate ethnic group.** Even
where there are sizable Puerto Rican populations--as in
Florida, Illinois, and California--they represent only a
minority within the larger Hispanic minority that is mainly
composed of Chicanos and, in Florida, of Cubans. In these
states, the census does not put Puerto Ricans in a separate
category from the other Spanish-surname residents.

---

*See the following "General, Social and Economic Char-
acteristics," volumes of the 1970 census for each state;
New York (PC1-C-34); New Jersey (PC1-C-32); and Pennsylvania (PC1-C40).

**Some data on Puerto Ricans at the state and city level
are available in the1970 Census Report "Puerto Ricans in
the United States," PC(2)-1E.

It is therefore impossible to examine the socioeconomic
status of Puerto Ricans on a state and local level on the
basis of Census Bureau reports alone. Data might be available from state and city agencies (particularly in the
fields of education, labor, and welfare), but even these
sources are unlikely to treat Puerto Ricans as a separate
ethnic group in states and cities where they have little
statistical weight.

Because of these limitations, this section on the
state and local population profile of Puerto Ricans on
the mainland concentrates on those states (New York, New
Jersey, and Pennsylvania) where comparisons with other
ethnic groups are available. Briefer consideration is
given to the Midwestern states of Illinois and Ohio and
the New England states of Connecticut and Massachusetts.

Comparisons of Puerto Ricans with whites and blacks
in a given area are essential because of the different
living conditions and costs in different areas. To say,
for example, that a Puerto Rican family in Buffalo earns
$6,000 a year while a family in New York City earns $8,000
is meaningless unless one compares these figures with the
median of the total population in those areas.

In certain respects, the state and city statistics
are particularly valuable because they bring to light certain population differences among Puerto Ricans that are
hidden in the averaging out of national statistics. Socioeconomic characteristics for Puerto Ricans in large cities
of the United States generally conform to the nationwide
figures, showing high levels of unemployment and poverty,
low levels of education, and low median age. But a closer
look, on a city-by-city basis (see Table 63, for example),
reveals small pockets of Puerto Rican populations that are
exceptions to the rule, indicating that Puerto Ricans in
the United States are not as homogeneous as the stereo-
types attributed to them. In West New York, New Jersey,
for example, a Puerto Rican community of 1,167 persons has
a median family income of $8,369 per year, and in Clifton,
New Jersey, an even smaller group of 374 Puerto Ricans has
family incomes averaging $9,900 per year, while just a few
miles away, in Newark, the 27,443 Puerto Ricans have average family incomes of $4,983.

Whether the more affluent Puerto Ricans worked their
way up and out of the inner cities or whether they were
middle-class migrants to begin with are questions not re-
solved by the Census Bureau reports. In any case, such
questions about the paths of Puerto Rican mobility in the
United States are raised by examining the state and city

statistics. This area of social mobility is but one example of the many areas of possible investigation suggested by the data on Puerto Ricans presented according to residence in various states and cities in this chapter and in Chapter 5.

NEW YORK STATE

The 872,471 Puerto Ricans in New York State represented 4.8 percent of the state's total population, according to the 1970 census. While one of every five white families and about one of every ten black families in New York State had incomes of from $15,000 to $25,000 per year, only one of every 22 Puerto Rican families was in this upper-middle income bracket. At the other end of the spectrum, 29 percent of Puerto Rican families lived in poverty, compared with 20 percent of blacks and 7 percent of whites (see Table 38).

Only in Nassau and Suffolk counties, which have a combined Puerto Rican population of under 25,000 persons, does median family income exceed $10,000 per year; this is double the figure for the bulk of the families who live in the Bronx, Kings, and New York counties (see Table 39). As one might expect, the three counties where Puerto Ricans have higher education levels (Nassau, Queens, and Suffolk) also have the populations with the highest family incomes.

New York City SMSA

Puerto Ricans are scattered throughout New York State (see Table 40), but the largest concentration by far is in New York City (811,843 persons) and the number swells (845,775) if one includes the surrounding urban areas that comprise the New York City Standard Metropolitan Statistical Area (SMSA), where Puerto Ricans represent 7.3 percent of the population (see Table 41).

Puerto Ricans have made a substantial impact upon population trends in New York City. Between 1960 and 1970, population in most major Eastern and Midwestern cities dropped (Cleveland by 14.3 percent, Detroit by 4.5 percent, Chicago by 5.2 percent, Baltimore by 3.5 percent, and Philadelphia by 2.7 percent) whereas Western cities such as Los Angeles, Dallas, and Houston enjoyed large gains. New York City's population rose by 113,000 persons (or 1.5 percent) because the growth of black and Puerto Rican communities more than offset the white exodus. Between 1950 and 1970, while New York City's population remained relatively stable, the number of blacks doubled to 1.8 million and the number of Puerto Ricans tripled to above 800,000.

The pace of change quickened during the past two decades. Between 1950 and 1960, New York City's white population dropped by 6.7 percent, and fell even more sharply, 8.9 percent, between 1960 and 1970. The black population grew by 47 percent in the first decade and 62 percent in the second. The pattern of Puerto Rican growth was more complex. Between 1950 and 1960, it soared by 150 percent. But in the next decade it grew by only 32 percent, indicating a shift away from New York City, since the nationwide growth rate for Puerto Ricans during that same period was 61 percent (see Table 42).

In addition to Puerto Ricans, the 1970 census found more than half a million other Hispanic people living in the New York metropolitan area, but the true number is much higher. The federal government estimates that more than 1 million illegal aliens reside in New York, and that 75 percent are Hispanic (mainly Colombians, Dominicans, Argentinians, Ecuadorians, and citizens of different Central American republics). The New York City borough of Queens alone holds an estimated 400,000 Hispanics (including Puerto Ricans), and it is believed that some 80,000 Colombians, Argentinians, and Ecuadorians live in the Jackson Heights-Elmhurst-Corona section of Queens. "Most new Latin arrivals come here illegally," says a recent news report, and many try to pass as Puerto Ricans (who are U.S. citizens by birthright) so that they may get a Social Security card and qualify for better jobs.[1] An official with the Migration Division of the Puerto Rican government office in Manhattan reports that the situation has become so "drastic" that Puerto Ricans are being issued special laminated ID cards, certifying that they were born in Puerto Rico and are therefore U.S. citizens. However, he adds, many other Hispanics come to the office, often bearing falsified birth certificates, seeking these ID cards.[2] Without legal status as either citizens or resident aliens, these Hispanics are often victimized by employers and landlords, who realize that these illegal immigrants risk deportation if they complain. They are also politically disenfranchised and "exist virtually as civic nonpersons."[3]

While Puerto Ricans in New York City have full legal status as citizens, their participation in the educational and economic life of the city is far weaker than their population share of 7.3 percent. They have only 2.2 percent of the college students, 1.4 percent of the professional workers, one-half of 1 percent of the doctors and dentists, seven-tenths of 1 percent of the teachers, 1.9 percent of the managers and administrators, and (in the only category where they are overrepresented) more than 13 percent of the factory workers (see Table 41 again).

New York City has 261,956 Puerto Rican students, but only 1,145 Puerto Rican teachers, a ratio of 228 to 1 (the ratio of students to teachers in the city population is about 20 to 1).

Median income for Puerto Rican families is $5,666, about $30 a week less than for black families, and $100 a week lower than the figure for all families in the area.

Nearly 8 percent of Puerto Rican families in the New York City SMSA had incomes below $1,000 per year, and only 5 percent earned $15,000 or more per year. A better appreciation of these figures is gained by the fact that a New York City family with three children needs about $11,300 a year to achieve an intermediate standard of living, and $7,081 per year to achieve a lower acceptable standard of living (see Table 43).

In 1970, the federal government defined poverty as an income of $3,740 or less for a family of four, or $4,415 for a family of five. That year, 399,000 black and 283,000 Puerto Rican New Yorkers were in poverty, and an additional 130,000 blacks and 30,000 Puerto Ricans were in the near-poor category, with incomes only 25 percent above the poverty definition. This means that 32 percent of the blacks and 45 percent of the Puerto Ricans in the city were either poor or near-poor.[4] A U.S. census survey of seven low-income areas in New York City (taken between October 1970 and March 1971) showed that unemployment among Puerto Ricans was substantially above that of blacks (10.6 percent for Puerto Rican males and 8.5 percent for black males; 12 percent for Puerto Rican women and 7.2 percent for black women).

Much of the dispute over the alleged (and quite apparent) undercount of Puerto Ricans in the United States centers upon New York City. The 1970 census found only 811,800 Puerto Ricans in the city, but a survey by the Center for Social Research of CUNY found more than 1 million. Thus, depending upon whose figures one believes, Puerto Ricans represent from 10.3 percent to 12.9 percent of the city's population (see Table 44).

Both surveys agree that the highest concentrations of Puerto Ricans are in the boroughs of the Bronx (21.5 to

25.9 percent of the borough's population), Manhattan (12 to 17.3 percent), and Brooklyn (10.4 to 12 percent).

Even after the influx of minority groups, whites still represent 65 percent of the city's population. But the picture differs in the public schools, where only 38 percent of the students are white. On the other hand, 23 percent are Puerto Rican, reflecting the youthful nature of the Hispanic population (see Table 45).

Since 1960, the Puerto Rican and black shares of public school enrollment have grown rapidly (see Table 46). In the Bronx, for example, 43 percent of students in elementary grades and 53 percent of those in vocational schools are Puerto Rican. In Manhattan they have about a one-third share at all school levels. Even in Queens, where Puerto Ricans have only 3 percent of the elementary, intermediate and academic high school students, they have 15 percent of enrollment in vocational high schools (see Table 47).

Citywide, Puerto Ricans have 33 percent of the enrollment in vocational high schools, but only 15 percent in the academic high schools, a guarantee that their share of future college enrollment will be correspondingly low. However, between 1961 and 1970, there has been dramatic improvement in Puerto Rican enrollment in academic high schools from 5.5 percent to 15 percent (see Table 48).

There is still a huge gap among the educational achievements of white, black, and Puerto Rican persons in New York City. Between 1960 and 1970, white high school graduates increased from 40 to 51 percent of the white adult population. For blacks the figure jumped from 31 to 40 percent, and for Puerto Ricans from 13 to 20 percent. In the same decade, the number of white college graduates went from 9.4 to 13 percent, while blacks remained steady at 4 percent and Puerto Ricans climbed from under 1 percent to 1 percent (see Table 49).

During the same period, family income for whites grew by 26 percent, compared with 24 percent for blacks and only 13 percent for Puerto Ricans, meaning that both minority groups (during a period of vigorous economic growth) fell behind in relative terms. In 1963, for example, black families earned 72 percent of white family income and Puerto Rican families earned 58 percent of the white level. By 1969, blacks had fallen to 64 percent, and Puerto Ricans dropped to 50 percent (see Table 50).

Although Puerto Ricans comprise at least 10 percent of New York City's population, their political clout is far less. According to one informed observer, Puerto

Ricans "do not have a concentrated base of power, but are spread throughout the city"; also, "in areas where they make up the majority of the population, they are either apathetic politically or run opposing Puerto Rican candidates who split the bloc vote and allow a minority of the voters to put their candidate across." Figures published by the Citizens Voter Registration Campaign in 1969 showed that of about 435,000 Puerto Ricans of voting age only 131,000 were registered. A voter registration drive in black and Puerto Rican areas that year drew "only a handful" of new potential voters.[5]

The problem of geographic fragmentation of the Puerto Rican vote has been aggravated by urban renewal projects and gerrymandering tactics by those now holding political power.

On the issue of voter apathy, Joseph Monserrat, chairman of New York City's Board of Education, said that most Puerto Ricans of voting age were born and raised on the island and, for linguistic and cultural reasons, do not identify with local issues and candidates. He maintains that a second group, born in Puerto Rico but raised and educated in New York, has many members active in politics. The third group, born in the United States, is, in its majority, too young to vote. "As these youngsters reach voting age," said Monserrat, "I think we are going to see a different political style, one which reflects the urban reality and which is different than that of their parents."[6]

Between 1960 and 1971, the number of employed men in New York City dropped by 10.5 percent. Between June 1973 and June 1974, New York City lost 41,000 jobs, while surrounding suburban areas gained 35,000 jobs; 15,700 of the jobs lost to the city were in manufacturing (a prime source of employment for Puerto Rican males). Other key losses were in wholesale and retail trade (11,600 jobs) and transport and utilities (8,000 jobs).[7]

Since the jobless rate in Puerto Rico is high and climbing, there will be continuous pressure for Puerto Ricans in New York City to migrate elsewhere.

This gradual exodus has been taking place during the past decade. When it has not been a search for jobs, it has been a quest for better living conditions by those who can afford to do so.

Yonkers

Yonkers, for example, which lies just north of New York City, has a small Puerto Rican population and a higher

percentage of persons with middle-income status. Yonkers
has 2,630 Puerto Ricans with a median age of 20.9 years.
The 659 Puerto Rican families in Yonkers had a median annual income of only $7,227. Unemployment was 6.9 percent
for adult males and 11.2 percent for women. But 88 of the
840 employed Puerto Ricans living in Yonkers (more than
10 percent) were in the professional-technical class including six doctors and dentists and 24 teachers, 34 percent of the adult males and 35 percent of the adult women
were high school graduates.

Urban Balance of New York SMSA

Even closer to middle-class status were the 29,024
Puerto Ricans living in the urban balance of the New York
City SMSA (urban fringe areas that do not include New York
City, Levittown, Mount Vernon, New Rochelle, White Plains,
or Yonkers).

About 54 percent of the Puerto Ricans ages 3 to 34
years in these areas were enrolled in school, including
2,134 high school students and 409 college students. Adult
males had 10.3 median school years completed and 35 percent were high school graduates. Women had 10.7 school
years and 40.5 percent were high school graduates.

Unemployment was only 2.4 percent for men and 4.8 percent for women. Of the 9,958 employed persons, 932 were
in professional-technical jobs. Among the 5,985 Puerto
Rican families in these areas, median income was $10,092
and per capita income was $2,393 (compared with $1,739 in
New York City). There were 999 families with incomes of
from $15,000 to $25,000 per year, 150 families earning
$25,000 to $50,000 and 21 families earning above $50,000
per year.

Of these families only 11.9 percent were beneath the
poverty line (compared with 30.4 percent in New York City).
Of the 6,091 households, 3,430 lived in their own homes,
which had a mean value of $25,079.

Long Island

Between 1960 and 1970, the Puerto Rican population on
Long Island more than doubled (from 11,500 to 24,403) and
now accounts for nearly 1 percent of that area's population.
Many of the early Puerto Rican migrants were attracted by
jobs in Suffolk County's two large state mental institu-

tions (Pilgrim State and Central Islip), which may account for the fact that although Suffolk County is farther from New York City than Nassau County it has the larger Puerto Rican population (17,000 to 7,000).

The 1970 census counted at least 400 Puerto Ricans in eight Long Island communities (Brentwood, Central Islip, Deer Park, Glen Cove, Huntington Station, Long Beach, North Great River, and Patchogue), with numbers ranging from 435 in Huntington Station to 1,666 in Central Islip.

Roughly 10 percent of the Puerto Rican families on Long Island live below the poverty level (compared with 28 percent in New York City) and median family income is above $10,000 per year (compared with $5,500 in New York City). Levels of education are higher and unemployment lower than in New York City (see Table 51).

While economic conditions are far better, pressures to conform in a mainly white community are quite strong. A teacher in Brentwood, for example, told a visitor that many Puerto Rican students in the public schools were undergoing "identity crises" and sometimes avoided being identified as Puerto Ricans. Another teacher said that some Puerto Rican students claimed they were Italian, and others resented being spoken to in Spanish.[8]

Buffalo

In addition to the Puerto Rican populations in and around New York City, there are smaller communities scattered throughout the state, such as those in Buffalo, Rochester, Syracuse, Dunkirk, Utica, and Newburgh.

The first Puerto Ricans came to the Buffalo area in the late 1940s and early 1950s to pick crops in the fields of western New York. Some of them secured permanent jobs in the railyards, steel mills, and factories near Lake Erie. By 1960, the census showed 2,907 persons of Puerto Rican birth or parentage in Erie County. By 1970, the census counted 5,532 Puerto Ricans in the Buffalo SMSA (see Table 52), although the figure may be higher. For example, the 1970 census shows 13,133 persons "of Spanish origin or descent" in that area. Subtracting the Puerto Ricans already identified, as well as the Mexicans, Cubans, and other Latin Americans who were also identified, there remain nearly 5,000 persons "of Spanish origin or descent" whose ethnic origins were not specified. By 1970, more than one-fourth of the students in elementary schools on Buffalo's lower west side had Spanish surnames.[9] As shown

in Table 52 , more than half of the Puerto Ricans in Buffalo
were under age 18. The average Puerto Rican adult had only
eight years of schooling, while the average area resident
had a high school diploma. Unemployment among Puerto Rican
males was 9.7 percent compared with 9.2 percent for blacks
and 4.4 percent for the total population. Family income
for Puerto Ricans was $6,638 compared with $6,955 for
black families and $10,430 for all area families. Per
capita income was even lower, because of the larger size
of the Puerto Rican family, and the lesser number of wage
earners per family. More than 27 percent of the Puerto
Rican families were under the poverty level compared with
24 percent for blacks and 5 percent for all area families.
Only about 12 percent of the Puerto Rican families lived
in their own homes (mean value $11,923), compared with 15
percent of the blacks (mean value $12,094) and 57 percent
of area residents (mean value $19,776).

NEW JERSEY

New Jersey in 1970 had a population of 7.1 million
persons, including 310,476 persons of Hispanic origin;
of these, 135,676 were Puerto Rican. Nearly 96 percent of
the Puerto Ricans live in urban areas, compared with 88
percent of the state's residents (see Table 53).

The state's largest Puerto Rican community is in Newark (27,443), followed by Jersey City (16,194), Paterson
(11,927), Hoboken (10,047), Passaic (6,826), Perth Amboy
(6,606), and Camden (6,526)--see Table 54.

Puerto Ricans represent less than 2 percent of New
Jersey's population, but in Hoboken more than 22 percent
of the residents are Puerto Rican. Other areas of high
Puerto Rican concentration are: Perth Amboy (17 percent),
Passaic (12.4 percent), Vineland (9.9 percent), Dover (9.7
percent), Paterson (8.2 percent), Newark (7.1 percent),
Camden (6.3 percent), Jersey City (6.2 percent), and Lake-
wood (6.2 percent). Since even the Census Bureau has ad-
mitted to undercounting Puerto Ricans, these figures are
probably quite conservative.

(It is beyond the scope of this survey, but it would
be helpful to study at what point a critical mass is
achieved, either via the sheer size of the Puerto Rican
population in a given town, or by virtue of its representing a high percentage of a town's population. By critical
mass, we mean that point at which a minority group makes a
strong impact upon the social, economic, and political life

of a community. For this reason, towns such as Hoboken, Perth Amboy, Passaic, and others with high Puerto Rican concentrations merit further detailed study with respect to the emergence of political leadership, the establishment of community service organizations, the impact upon public schools and upon the life style of the town, and so forth.)

With a median age of 18.9 years, the Puerto Rican in New Jersey is far younger than the average resident, whose median age is 31.4 years. Puerto Rican women marry younger (52 percent of the Puerto Rican women ages 15 to 24 had been married compared with 31 percent of the black women and 29 percent of the white women) and tend to have more children (see Table 55).

Of the Puerto Rican families in New Jersey 78 percent include children under age 18 compared with 53 percent of the white families and 65 percent of the black families; 51 percent of the Puerto Rican families have children under age 6, more than double the rate for white families. Also, 19 percent of the Puerto Rican families are headed by a woman compared with 9 percent of white families and 29 percent of black families. Among those families headed by a woman, the Puerto Rican family head is far more likely to be supporting young children than are her counterparts in white or black families (see Table 56).

The Puerto Rican male in New Jersey has completed a median of 8.4 school years compared with 12.2 years for whites and 10.2 years for blacks. Educational achievement is roughly similar for women of the three groups (see Table 57).

These figures, however, do not adequately demonstrate the sharp differences in education. For example, while only 4.3 percent of white adults and 8.9 percent of black adults in New Jersey have less than five years of elementary school training, this is the case for 23.4 percent of Puerto Ricans. And, while 12.5 percent of the white adults are college graduates, only 4.1 percent of the blacks and 2 percent of the Puerto Ricans have finished college. Among persons ages 18 to 24, only 28 percent of the Puerto Ricans have graduated from high school, compared with 68 percent of whites and 54 percent of blacks. In this age group, only one-half of 1 percent of the Puerto Ricans hold college degrees compared with 8 percent of the whites and 2 percent of the blacks (see Table 58).

Enrollment figures in New Jersey schools suggest that Puerto Ricans will lag behind in education for some years to come. In the 7-to-15-year-old bracket, school enroll- ment among Puerto Ricans compares quite favorably with

47

that of whites and blacks, with all three groups achieving
90 percent or higher enrollment. But far fewer Puerto
Ricans are enrolled in preschool programs or remain in
school once they reach age 16. For example, in the 16-to-
17-year-old bracket, while 93 percent of the whites and 84
percent of the blacks are still in school, only 71 percent
of the Puerto Ricans are enrolled. In the 18-to-19-year-
old bracket, 60 percent of the whites, 45 percent of the
blacks and only 37 percent of the Puerto Ricans remain in
school (see Table 59).

Among males in the 16-to-21-year-old bracket, 46 percent of the Puerto Ricans are not attending school and do
not hold high school diplomas, compared with only 11 percent of the whites and 26 percent of the blacks (see Table
60).

A higher percentage of Puerto Rican males in New Jersey are either working or actively seeking work (82 percent) than whites (80 percent) or blacks (75 percent), but
despite this high participation in the labor force, unemployment among Puerto Rican males is 6 percent compared
with 2.8 percent for whites and 6 percent for blacks. For
women, Puerto Ricans have a lower labor force participation
rate than whites or blacks, and a higher unemployment rate
(see Table 61).

The white family in New Jersey earns nearly double
the income of the Puerto Rican family (respective median
incomes are $10,157 and $5,789). Also, while 4.8 percent
of white families and 18.9 percent of black families have
incomes below the poverty line, more than 24 percent of
Puerto Rican families are in this impoverished status (see
Table 62).

Between 1960 and 1970 the Puerto Rican population in
New Jersey more than doubled from 55,351 to 135,676, and
the number of Puerto Ricans born in the United States more
than tripled from 15,572 to 51,419. This birth increase
caused a drop in median age from 20.5 years to 18.9 years.

During that decade, there were slight gains in level
of education, school enrollment and employment, and rather
dramatic gains in income. The median income of male wage
earners, for example, jumped from $2,961 in 1960 to $5,446
in 1970 (see Table 63). But nationwide statistics, cited
earlier, show that whites and blacks in the United States
have made even more dramatic gains in income.

48

City-by-City Differences

While the statewide figures for New Jersey accurately portray the socioeconomic status of the majority of the Puerto Rican residents, they do not show the rather considerable differences that exist in various communities.

Median age, for example, ranged from a high of 24.2 years for Puerto Ricans in Carteret to a low of 15.2 years in Atlantic City. Puerto Ricans in New Brunswick averaged only 6 years of schooling, while those in Irvington had 9.8 years. In Clifton, 36 percent of the Puerto Rican adults had a high school education compared with only 2.1 percent in New Brunswick. In Dover, 94.7 percent of adult males were in the labor force, compared with only 71.9 percent in Camden. Unemployment ranged from a high of 11.7 percent in Long Branch to virtually zero in towns such as Carteret and Hammonton. Median family income for Puerto Ricans was $8,683 in Plainfield and only $3,266 in Atlantic City. Virtually no Puerto Ricans in Carteret received public assistance, while 38.4 percent of those in Camden did.

Some of the towns where Puerto Ricans score higher in key socioeconomic indexes are apparently suburban in nature and are inhabited by Puerto Rican families who have long been members of the middle class, or who have recently attained that status and moved from poor inner-city environments. On the other hand, some other towns may (by virtue of size, location, and employment opportunities) provide more favorable conditions for a migrant family to survive and prosper. This is another area that deserves deeper study.

In an attempt to discern patterns, Table 64 indicates with a small box (□) those three or four towns where Puerto Ricans score worst in key socioeconomic indexes and marks with an asterisk (*) those three or four communities where they score best. By doing so there emerges a clear correlation among low median age, low level of schooling, low income, and high levels of poverty and dependence upon public assistance.

Puerto Ricans in Atlantic City, for example, had the lowest median age (15.2 years), were in the bottom half with respect to high school education (15.9 percent), had the lowest per capita income ($998), and had the highest percentage of families beneath the poverty level.

On the other hand, Carteret had the highest median age (24.2 years), the fourth best per capita income ($2,350), and had lower percentages of families on welfare

49

(10.8 percent) and families below the poverty line (17.6 percent).

The city with the most asterisks (denoting favorable scores) was West New York, with a high median age (23 years), a high percentage of high school graduates (33.1 percent), low unemployment (2.4 percent), and high income ($8,369 per family and $2,421 per capita).

Other cities where Puerto Ricans scored high were Clifton, Dover, and Plainfield. Cities where they scored low were Atlantic City, Newark, Camden, Vineland, and New Brunswick.

Another area that deserves serious study is the birth-place of the Puerto Rican migrant. It is often surprising to find how many residents in a particular U.S. town come from the same barrio, town, or part of Puerto Rico. This is apparently due to the efficient word-of-mouth communications system between relatives and friends. Despite its small size, Puerto Rico is quite varied in many respects with both rural and suburban areas. For many years, the nature of work was far different on the coastal plains (slaves cutting cane on large plantations, later replaced by serf-like freemen) than it was in the remote mountain areas (small family farms specializing mainly in coffee, tobacco, and fruits and vegetables). Economic systems profoundly affect cultural attitudes, which are passed on for generations. It would be helpful to see to what extent these attitudes have been preserved in the United States, and whether they might account for some of the differences in socioeconomic achievement.

Now we shall examine in greater detail the Puerto Rican populations in a few New Jersey communities. Much of the data in this narrative and accompanying tables are taken from different sections in the 1970 U.S. census volume "General Social and Economic Characteristics, New Jersey," PC(1)-C32 N.J. (especially from Tables 81 through 116).

Newark

Newark is perhaps a classic example of several large, decaying urban areas in the United States whose inner cities are occupied mainly by low-income blacks and Puerto Ricans. Newark is the first large city in the northern United States where blacks achieved a numerical majority with 54.2 of the total population of 382,374 in 1970. The 27,443 Puerto Ricans accounted for 7.1 percent of the city's population in 1970.

In August 1967, following widespread black rioting in Newark, a Select Committee on Civil Disorders appointed by Governor Richard J. Hughes reported that the rising needs of the city's Spanish-speaking people were "being neglected as we grapple with the more massive pressures from the Negro population."

According to Gustav Heningburg, head of the Greater Newark Urban Coalition, "for all intents and purposes--politically, economically and socially--the Puerto Rican community has been invisible. . . . Until Sunday . . . nobody had taken them seriously."[10]

The Sunday referred to occurred during the Labor Day weekend of 1974 when an incident between police and Puerto Ricans at a Hispanic festival in Branch Brook Park grew into a full-scale riot, lasting a few days and resulting in the deaths of two Puerto Rican youths, numerous injuries and arrests, and widespread property damage. It has since been widely commented that numerous root causes were responsible for the rioting.

Here, according to 1970 census figures, are some of the possible root causes. Median family income citywide was only $6,191--$5,634 for blacks and $4,983 for Puerto Ricans. On a per capita basis, income for Puerto Ricans was even lower because of larger family size. The citywide per capita income figure was $2,498--$2,077 for blacks and $1,546 for Puerto Ricans. Very few Puerto Rican families lived in homes of their own, and--despite their low incomes--they paid rentals almost equal to the citywide average (see Table 65).

Although Puerto Ricans represented 7.1 percent of Newark's population, they held only a 1.2 share of the professional and technical jobs (150 out of 11,552). None of the 595 physicians and dentists residing in the city was Puerto Rican.* Only eight of the 2,577 teachers were Puerto Rican (about one-third of 1 percent, although about 7.6 percent of the city's students were Puerto Rican).

The Newark metropolitan area (including Newark and adjacent Bloomfield, East Orange, Elizabeth, and Irvington) holds 39,967 Puerto Ricans, about 2 percent of the area's population. About 336 Puerto Ricans from this area are

---

*The Newark Star-Ledger of September 13, 1974 (p. 18) reported that in 1970, there were "perhaps two Puerto Rican dentists in the entire state of New Jersey," and only one living in the five northern counties of the state, where there were 116,000 Puerto Rican residents.

enrolled in college (about one-half of 1 percent of the
area enrollment). Blacks, who represent 19 percent of the
area's population, have 10 percent of the area's college
students. There are only 403 Puerto Rican professional
and technical workers among a total of 130,640 in the area.
This includes 21 doctors and dentists, compared with 230
blacks and 6,472 for the general population; there are
only 37 Puerto Rican teachers, compared with 2,597 black
teachers and a total of 27,766 teachers.

Following the Labod Day 1974 riots, the press paid
much more attention to the Puerto Rican situation in Newark.
It was reported that unemployment rates for Puerto Ricans
in Newark were about 27 percent, with an estimated 30 percent of the community dependent upon some form of welfare,
and a high school dropout rate of 42 percent.[11] It was
further reported that only 1 or 2 percent of federal money
coming into the city to deal with the poor was being chan-
neled into the Puerto Rican community, which has about 30
percent of the city's poor.[12] There were further horror
stories about the plight of Puerto Ricans in Newark. A
survey by a Puerto Rican professor at Rutgers University
was quoted, showing that of 200 Puerto Rican mothers who
were interviewed, only 12 had received prenatal care.[13] It
was further stated by a New Jersey Department of Education
official that more than one-fourth of the nearly 90,000
Hispanic students in the state were "doomed to failure, because the system is teaching them in a language they don't
understand." The official added that Puerto Rican students
were dropping out at a rate three times higher than whites
in New Jersey and half again as often as blacks.[14] It was
also reported that only 4,000 (under 2 percent) of New
Jersey's 187,000 college students had Spanish surnames and
that there were only 40 Hispanics engaged in graduate work
in New Jersey's 15 colleges. But the main targets of crit-
icism were Newark's public schools where some Puerto Rican
students are listed as retarded because of language diffi-
culties, while others are promoted despite their academic
deficiencies. In one Newark high school, an official found
ten Puerto Rican students who spoke no English at all, yet
had been passed along, from grade to grade. A Puerto Rican
women who works as a community relations specialist with
Rutgers University said: "I honestly believe that if the
Newark school system burned to the ground tomorrow, it
wouldn't really have much of an impact on our children."[15]

After the Labor Day riots, the Newark city government
formed committees and launched studies to investigate ac-
cusations of police brutality and to look into the root

causes of the unrest. Two weeks after the riot the only
tangible concession made to alleviate these root causes
was a promise made by two New Jersey dental colleges who
announced that they hoped to enroll 12 Puerto Ricans on
scholarship by September 1976.

Jersey City

Nearby Jersey City conforms roughly to the Newark pattern, although blacks represent 21 percent of the city's
population, and the 16,194 Puerto Ricans have a 6.2 percent
share.

It is interesting to note, as is the case in several
cities, that Puerto Rican males in New Jersey have a very
high rate of labor force participation; that is, they are
either employed or actively seeking work (see Table 65).
In fact, their participation rate is higher than the city
average. However, their unemployment rate (6.5 percent)
is both higher than the city average (3.8 percent) and the
black average (4.8 percent).

Only 4.4 percent of the Puerto Rican workers occupied
professional and technical jobs compared with a city average of 10.4 percent. Only 12.8 percent of the Puerto Rican
workers occupied clerical jobs compared with a city average
of 26 percent. On the other hand, 35 percent of the Puerto
Ricans worked as factory operatives compared with 17 percent
of the city's employed.

Family income for Puerto Ricans was 72 percent of the
city average, but per capita income (because of large family size) was only 54 percent. Partly for this reason,
25 percent of Puerto Rican families were beneath the poverty line, compared with 10 percent for the entire city
and 19 percent for blacks. Only 155 of the 3,715 Puerto
Rican families in Jersey City lived in their own homes.
The vast majority rented paying $95 per month, a figure
only $13 less (per month) than the citywide average, de-
spite their far lower incomes.

Paterson

Paterson, an old industrial center, conforms to the
Newark-Jersey City pattern. About 27 percent of the city's
144,835 residents are black. The 11,927 Puerto Ricans represent 8.2 percent of Paterson's population (see Table 67).

Nearly one-third of Paterson's residents are high
school graduates compared with only one-seventh of the
city's Puerto Ricans. Because of this, and due to language
handicaps, only 71 of the city's 4,804 professional-technical jobs are filled by Puerto Ricans. Of the city's 215
physicians and dentists, and 1,159 teachers, none are
Puerto Rican (nearly 10 percent of the city's students are
Puerto Rican).

Only 74 of the 2,643 Puerto Rican families live in
their own homes. Those who live in apartments pay a mean
gross rental of $121 (per month), higher than the city
average, although family income for Puerto Ricans is $5,988,
compared with a citywide figure of $7,088.

Hoboken, Union City, and
West New York

There is a somewhat different situation in the smaller
towns of Hoboken, Union City, and West New York, which face
Manhattan along the western banks of the Hudson River.

In Hoboken, Puerto Ricans represent nearly one-fourth
of the total population of 45,390 (see Table 68), and an
even higher number according to undercount allegations.
Hoboken is primarily a blue-collar town, and the educational level of the Puerto Rican resident is not far below
that of the city average. The gap is also smaller in
terms of unemployment (5.3 percent for all males and 6.3
percent for Puerto Rican males), and median family income
($7,786 for all families and $5,154 per Puerto Rican family). Even in Hoboken, however, there are sharp contrasts.
About 195 (8.1 percent) of the Puerto Rican families have
incomes under $1,000 per year compared with 503 (4.4 per-
cent) of all families in Hoboken. Only 48 Puerto Rican
families (2 percent) earn more than $15,000 per year, com-
pared with 1,395 Hoboken families (12.4 percent).

One of the most interesting aspects of Hoboken is that
Puerto Ricans are the largest single minority group in the
city since there are only 1,860 blacks. This suggests a
far different sociopolitical situation in terms of seeking
an equitable share of local power. In Hoboken, Puerto
Ricans are seeking to wrest their share of local power from
a long-entrenched white establishment.

There are somewhat similar situations in Union City
and West New York, small towns where Puerto Ricans represent 5.3 and 2.9 percent, respectively, of the population.
But in these towns there is a different force: other Hispanics, mainly Cubans, represent the largest minority

group. In Union City, for example (see Table 69), nearly 16,000 of the town's residents are of Cuban birth or parentage and 3,114 are Puerto Rican, with a scattering of other Hispanics from other American nations. In Union City, nearly half the residents consider Spanish as their mother tongue. While this Spanish-language ambience is likely to be more comforting to Puerto Ricans, they still occupy the lowest rung of the ladder in terms of education, employment, and income. The reasons why are not obscure. The majority of the Cubans were members of the middle class, part of the exodus from Cuba when Castro's regime took power in 1959. Most Puerto Ricans, on the other hand, came from the island's lowest economic group, in search of jobs and upward mobility. Thus, while Puerto Rican family income ($6,676) is not far below the city average ($7,464), only 20 of Union City's professional-technical workers are Puerto Rican, and in 1970 there were no Puerto Ricans among the city's 70 physicians and dentists and 366 teachers.

The situation is similar in West New York, a town of 40,666 residents, where 1,167 Puerto Ricans (2.9 percent of the total) reside together with 15,000 other Hispanic people, most of them Cuban (see Table 70). Median family income for Puerto Ricans ($8,539) is actually higher than the citywide figure ($7,988) but larger families cause per capita income among Puerto Ricans to be lower ($2,921) than the city average ($3,377). In West New York about 33 percent of the adult male Puerto Ricans are high school graduates, the same as the city average, and Puerto Ricans occupy about 2 percent of the professional-technical jobs (close to their population "weight") although none of the city's 267 teachers are Puerto Rican.

PENNSYLVANIA

The 44,535 Puerto Ricans in Pennsylvania represent less than one-half of 1 percent of the state's 10.7 million people, but their presence is more strongly felt since 95.8 percent of the Puerto Ricans live in the Philadelphia metropolitan area, and more than half (26,702) live within the city limits of Philadelphia (see Tables 71 and 72).

The median age for Puerto Ricans in Pennsylvania is only 16.1 years, about half the statewide figure. Only 18.9 percent of adult Puerto Ricans had a high school education, compared with 51.6 percent of all Pennsylvanians and 33.2 percent of the blacks in the state; 2.6 percent

of the Puerto Rican adults had college degrees, compared
with 9.1 percent for the total population and 3.4 percent
for blacks.

Of the 11,412 Puerto Rican adults who were employed,
630 were in professional-technical jobs including 39 engi-
neers, 31 doctors and dentists, and 150 teachers. Puerto
Rican families in the state had a median income of $6,255,
compared with a statewide figure of $9,734 and $7,169 for
blacks. Of the 9,219 Puerto Rican families, 479 (5.2 percent) earned from $15,000 to $25,000 a year; 30 families
(one-third of 1 percent) earned from $25,000 to $50,000 a
year; and 5 families earned $50,000 or more a year.

Of the Puerto Rican families in Pennsylvania, 23.1 percent received some form of public assistance, but an even
higher figure, 30.3 percent, were living below the poverty
line, and 41.3 percent were in a category defined as near
poverty, meaning that their incomes were scarcely above the
poverty level.

Puerto Ricans in Philadelphia were, on the average,
even poorer than their compatriots scattered through the
rest of the state. More than 48 percent of the Puerto
Rican families in metropolitan Philadelphia depended upon
some form of public assistance, compared with 44 percent
of blacks and 28 percent of the area's total population.
From these figures, one can readily see that poverty is
far from being a problem that affects only black and Hispanic peoples.

In actual number, there were 4,320 Puerto Rican families and 84,613 black families in metropolitan Philadelphia
receiving some form of public assistance. This leaves a
much larger remainder of 245,667 white American families
who receive some form of welfare aid.

NOTES

1. New York _Times_, August 18, 1974.
2. Personal interview, August 1974.
3. New York _Times_, August 18, 1974.
4. Ibid., August 17, 1972.
5. Alfonso Narvaez, in ibid., October 15, 1969.
6. New York _Times_, October 15, 1969.
7. Ibid., August 17, 1974.
8. Richard Greenspan, Puerto Ricans on Long Island
(New York: Aspira of New York, Inc., November 1971), 49 pp.
9. Buffalo Evening News, November 30, 1970.
10. New York _Times_, September 4, 1974, p. 48.

11. Ibid., September 9, 1974, p. 48.
12. Ibid.
13. Newark <u>Star-Ledger</u>, September 9, 1974, p. 1.
14. Ibid., September 11, 1974, p. 14.
15. Ibid.

5

CONNECTICUT

The number of Puerto Ricans in Connecticut grew from 15,247 to 37,609 between 1960 and 1970, according to the U.S. Census Bureau. This includes 24,000 migrants from Puerto Rico (median age 25.6 years) and 13,000 persons born in the United States to Puerto Rican parents (median age 7.1 years). The largest concentrations of Puerto Ricans in Connecticut were in the cities of Bridgeport (10,048) and Hartford (8,104) with clusters of from 500 to 5,000 in New Britain, New Haven, New London, Norwalk, Stamford, and Waterbury. Actual figures may be much higher. The New York _Times_ has estimated, for example, that "about 17 percent, or 25,000 of Bridgeport's residents are Puerto Rican."[1]

The case of Bridgeport, described in that _Times_ article, is illustrative of other areas in the state. For years Puerto Ricans had come from their native island (mainly from small rural communities like Aguadilla, Aguas Buenas, and Camuy) to pick Connecticut's tobacco and vegetable crops. A defense industry boom in Bridgeport in the early 1960s attracted thousands of Puerto Ricans (from New York City also) who took permanent jobs.

In recent years, however, the boom has subsided, and those hardest hit have been unskilled minority group members. In 1972, the office of the Mayor of Bridgeport estimated that citywide unemployment was 15 percent, with the jobless rate as high as 50 percent among Puerto Rican adults and 65 percent among Puerto Rican youths. To keep welfare rolls lower, the city's Welfare Department was offering free one-way airfare back to Puerto Rico for those without jobs.

As is the case on a nationwide basis, there are sharp differences in socioeconomic characteristics between native-born Puerto Ricans living in Connecticut and those born on the U.S. mainland (see Table 73). The latter have higher levels of education, income, and employment.

MASSACHUSETTS

The Puerto Rican population in Massachusetts grew from 5,217 in 1960 to 23,332 in 1970, according to the U.S. Census Bureau. The largest community is centered in Boston, where the census counted 7,335 in the city proper and 11,321 in the total metropolitan area. About 16,000 of the Puerto Ricans in Massachusetts were born in Puerto Rico (median age 22.6 years) while the remaining 7,000 were born in the United States (median age 5.9 years).

There are great differences in the life styles of the average resident of the greater Boston area and of the Puerto Ricans in that area. Perhaps the greatest is the median family income of $11,449 for all area residents as compared with $4,998 for Puerto Rican families (see Table 74).

In 1972 a study focusing upon Puerto Ricans in the area identified the "lack of adequate statistics on living conditions of Puerto Ricans" and "the language barrier" as two key problems in trying to improve conditions.[2]

Schoolchildren in the area, for example, are classified as white or nonwhite and Puerto Rican problems are not isolated from those of blacks or other minorities. As for the language barrier, says the study, "agencies in Boston and Springfield consistently had insufficient Spanish-speaking personnel, placing the Puerto Rican in the fringe area of a man who knows his needs but who can find no one to listen." The study estimated that at least 2,500 Puerto Rican children in Boston were not attending school, and that almost one-third of the Puerto Rican students at a junior high school in Springfield left before graduation.

Puerto Ricans are underrepresented even in areas where one would expect a better record. For example, there are 17 Massachusetts Community Action agencies that work with the Spanish-speaking community. Less than 8 percent of the 3,000 employees of these agencies are Spanish-speaking. In Springfield, the Concentrated Employment Program (which trains and develops basic working skills among the economically deprived) placed 150 persons in jobs in a three-year period. Only two of these persons were Spanish-speaking.

The study cites figures that nearly one-third of the Spanish-speaking children ages 6 through 17 living in Boston are not attending school, but the Boston School District has refused to conduct a citywide census to identify these children. In 1970, only seven Puerto Ricans were graduated from high school in Boston, and four of these students were from parochial schools.

In the smaller city of Springfield, there is an even higher concentration of Puerto Ricans. Of the total student enrollment of 31,216 in Springfield public schools, there are 1,172 Puerto Ricans in elementary grades and 313 in high school. In 1971, only 11 Puerto Ricans graduated from high school in Springfield, and none of these had taken college prep courses. A lack of bilingual school programs and a severe shortage of Spanish-speaking teachers and support personnel are important parts of the problem.

Another study, issued by the Mayor's Office of Human Rights in Boston,[3] states that of 12 schools in the Boston area some are one-half Puerto Rican and 3 are all Puerto Rican. This study claims that "not one guidance counselor" in the entire Boston school system can speak Spanish; that only 4 of the area's 5,800 teachers are Puerto Rican; and that the Boston schools have not even one secretary, administrator, clerical worker, reading specialist, science specialist, art specialist, truant officer, librarian, or even janitor from the Spanish-speaking community.

Of the estimated 5,000 Puerto Rican children in Boston's public schools, only 300 are exposed to some type of bilingual education program, and this meager victory was gained after a "long battle," says the report. In areas of Boston such as Roxbury, the South End, and Dorchester, the report continues, "there are more social agencies than grocery stores; and yet the community problems are still increasing." The major part of the budget of these agencies is to pay the salaries of administrative personnel; the money is not piped into the community itself.

ILLINOIS

The 1970 census showed a total of 88,244 Puerto Ricans living in the state of Illinois--more than double the number counted by the census in 1960. Of these, 53,664 were born in Puerto Rico and have a median age of 27.4 years. The remaining 34,580 were born on the U.S. mainland, and more than 31,000 are under the age of 18. In fact, the median age of those born on the mainland is 7.6 years.

The vast majority of the Puerto Ricans in Illinois
(87,168) live in Chicago and its surrounding urban area,
which has a total population of 6.9 million people including 1.2 million blacks (see Table 75). Chicago is the
residence of 327,168 Hispanic peoples, including more than
100,000 persons of Mexican birth or descent and more than
18,000 persons of Cuban birth or descent. But there are
also more than 114,000 persons who are identified by the
census only as "of the Spanish language," many of whom may
be Puerto Rican.

The 1930 census for Chicago showed only 2,742 Latin
Americans and only 8,777 in 1940. But an influx of Mexicans and Puerto Ricans occurred in the 1950s. Some Chi-
cago-area companies recruited Puerto Rican men to work in
factories, helped to transport them there, housed them in
unheated railroad boxcars or barracks, and then laid them
off as soon as business slackened. In one case, Puerto
Ricans were brought to work in an Illinois munitions plant
when the Korean War had just ended and the American workers had already left to take other jobs. Many Puerto
Ricans were laid off after receiving one paycheck, and were
stranded in Chicago.[4]

Table 75 shows the sharp differences among the total
Chicago population, blacks, and Puerto Ricans in such key
areas as education, employment, income, and poverty.

In 1971, it was estimated that the unemployment rate
among Chicago's Spanish-speaking residents was more than
six times the citywide average, and that in the Latin American barrios "one able-bodied man is unemployed for every
two who are employed." According to a study by Northwest-
ern University's Center for Urban Affairs,[5] unemployment
among young Latins was even higher, with 60 percent of
those under 20 unemployed.

Spanish-speaking workers in Chicago, according to the
study, earn an average of $106 a week, compared with $155
earned by the average Chicago factory worker.

Despite a Latin unemployment rate estimated at 30 percent compared with the citywide average of 4.8 percent, and
despite the fact that Latins constitute about 10 percent
of Chicago's population, Latins make up "far less than 10
percent of the families receiving welfare." The Illinois
Department of Public Aid found of 123,523 families receiving aid for dependent children, only 8,700 were Latins.[6]

The education picture is no less cheerful. It is estimated that 70 percent of all Puerto Rican and Mexican
children who enter Chicago's public schools never graduate
from high school. The city's Board of Education said that

61

in 1970 there were 44,631 public school students who spoke
only Spanish, but only one in five of these was in special
programs to learn English. There was only one Spanish-
speaking teacher in the Chicago school system for every
223 Spanish-speaking pupils. At the same time, there were
hundreds of teachers in Chicago who had graduated from
colleges in Mexico, Cuba, or Puerto Rico; they could speak
English but could not get teaching certificates in Chicago,
because the schools they attended were not accredited or
because they did not have the basic U.S. education course
credits. The Board of Education continues to hire American
teachers who have all the required course credits, but
cannot communicate with the students.[7]

The Latin community is almost without a voice in Chicago politics. In 1971, there was not one Puerto Rican
elected official throughout the state of Illinois; in Cook
County, only one Mexican-American held an elected office.

Urban renewal has been one of the most destructive
forces in encouraging community consciousness. Latin
leaders in Chicago are said to "live in fear of the urban
renewal bulldozer." A Latin American community is often
no longer established than the area is marked for renewal
of a conservation project. Most often, the new housing
is far too expensive for the low-income displaced residents.
Shortly after Puerto Ricans moved into the Lincoln Park
area, for example, federal money was used to transform old
houses into "fancy buildings for stock brokers, lawyers
and advertising executives," prompting one Latin leader
to say, "We have the unique distinction of living in the
fanciest neighborhoods, but before they become fancy."
In some crumbling areas, there have been waves of fires,
razing old buildings occupied by Latins, and one landlord
said he had been contacted by arsonists who offered, for
$500, to burn down his building so he could collect insur-
ance. In the Woodlawn area of Chicago alone, more than
30,000 residents were displaced by fires in a four-year period.[8]

However, out of 40,200 public housing units in Chicago, only 365 were occupied by Latins, despite the chronic
housing shortage.[9]

In June 1966, tough tactics by Chicago police in the
heavily Puerto Rican Northwest Side touched off a riot and
the action escalated when police dogs were brought in to
quell the crowd. After eight Puerto Ricans were shot,
many others (including two policemen) injured, and 48 ar-
rested, 500 helmeted police officers imposed martial law
on that sector of town. At the time, there were only 11

Spanish-speaking police officers in the Chicago Police Department, and not one of the 11 was assigned to the riot district.[10] Following the riot, more attention was paid to the Latin community's problems, but the basic ills remained.

In 1972, Puerto Rican columnist Jose Torres visited Chicago and commented, "while many blacks live in modern city projects, the Puerto Ricans live in the same tenements they lived in when they arrived 25 years ago. When they argue, it is among themselves. They live under the worst conditions in Chicago, but they know no enemy, no one to blame, no one to hate. . . . This place, as far as Puerto Ricans are concerned, reminds me of New York in 1954. . . . Puerto Ricans in Chicago seem to live in limbo. . . . We are years behind here in Chicago and there is only one thing I can yell: Help!"[11]

OHIO

Between 1960 and 1970, the Puerto Rican population in Ohio increased from 13,940 to 20,272. Of the latter amount, 9,849 were persons born on the mainland to Puerto Rican parents. Cleveland (8,104) and Lorain (6,031) were the areas of highest Puerto Rican concentration, but there were also Spanish-speaking communities ranging in size from 2,000 to 5,000 in Akron, Canton, Cincinnati, Columbus, Dayton, Lima, Toledo, and Youngstown.

There are some interesting contrasts between the Puerto Rican communities in Cleveland and Lorain, which may be a result of the relative sizes of these two cities, and of differing job opportunities (see Table 76).

In terms of education and school enrollment, Puerto Ricans in Cleveland rank higher than those in Lorain. But those in Lorain rank higher in terms of family stability (as measured by percent of families headed by a woman), male employment, and per capita income. Fewer families in Lorain are below the poverty level, and while less than one-third of the Cleveland families live in their own home, more than half of those in Lorain live in owner-occupied units.

According to a series of articles by Joseph Eszterhas in the Cleveland Plain Dealer, published between April 25-30, 1971, there were as many as 25,000 Puerto Ricans in the city of Cleveland, with most living in Wards 7 and 8 of the West Side, where more than 50 percent of the housing is substandard. The Puerto Ricans of Cleveland, says the series, are divided into three basic socioeconomic groups: "those who are affluent, who speak English fluently and have professional jobs . . . those who work in a factory or mill, have a median [sic] income and live in a lower-middle-class area . . . those who work in greenhouses and as cheap labor, speak little English and live in near-slum conditions on the . . . West Side."

Most of Cleveland's Puerto Ricans, said the series, "came . . . as cheap labor for the steel companies in the early 1950s." Politically, the Puerto Rican community is quite weak. Only 3,000 Puerto Ricans in Cleveland are registered voters and of 3,000 potential voters in one West Side ward, only 700 had voted in the previous election.

The education problem, as summed up by the Plain Dealer series, is aggravated by the fact that Cleveland, which has more than 4,000 Puerto Rican students, has no bilingual program, and only two Spanish-speaking teachers (neither of whom is Puerto Rican). The director of the Cleveland School Board's Latin Culture project, a non-Latin who speaks no Spanish, told the newspaper that there was "no need" for bilingual programs in the city's schools. He added that there was "no need" to recruit Puerto Rican teachers for his Latin Culture project, because his people were "doing a fine job."

NOTES

1. New York Times, June 11, 1972.
2. Report of the Massachusetts State Advisory Committee to the United States Commission on Civil Rights, "Issues of Concern to Puerto Ricans in Boston and Springfield," February 1972, 103 pp.
3. Alfredo de Jesus, Mayor's Office of Human Rights, Boston, Massachusetts, "Problems Faced by the Spanish Community in the City of Boston and the State of Massachusetts," May 13, 1971, 20 pp.
4. Chicago Daily News, August 1, 1971, p. 1.
5. Ibid., August 4, 1971, p. 1.
6. Ibid.
7. Ibid., August 2, 1971, p. 8.
8. Ibid., August 3, 1971, p. 1.
9. Ibid., August 1, 1971, p. 1.
10. New Republic, June 25, 1966, p. 7.
11. New York Post, October 7, 1972, p. 26.

III

LOOKING AHEAD:
PROSPECTS OF MAINLAND
PUERTO RICANS

6

A STRUGGLE
FOR SURVIVAL

Trying to predict the fortunes of an entire ethnic group--even for the near future--is a risky task because the complex interplay of the national economy, education, job opportunities, voter registration, and the gradual acquiring of political power will affect the outcome.

To begin with we must think within the framework of one important fact: since World War II the relative position of the poor in the United States has not gotten any better. The bottom 20 percent of all families had 5.1 percent of the nation's income in 1947 and had almost the same amount in 1972--5.4 percent. At the top, the richest 20 percent had 43.3 percent of the income in 1947 and 41.4 percent in 1972.[1] Thus, it is a fair assumption that unless there is major change in income distribution for all income groups in the United States, the possibility of dramatic improvement for the Puerto Rican community as a whole is not very promising. Keeping in mind this inequitable income distribution for the entire society, one can only speculate on how much Puerto Ricans can improve their socioeconomic lot under these circumstances. A few observations:

• The Puerto Rican community was so young in 1970 that it is difficult to determine what will happen when its younger members enter the labor market.

• Puerto Ricans are very urban, and a great number of jobs have shifted to suburban locations in recent years, reducing work opportunities in the cities. In a survey of America's 15 largest metropolitan areas for the years 1960 and 1970, it was found that the suburbs gained more than 3 million jobs (a gain of 44 percent), while the central cities lost 836,000 (a 7 percent decline).[2] In the New York metropolitan area, for example, while the number of jobs remained fairly constant during the decade, the number of jobs in the city dropped by 339,000. The decline has been even more rapid in the half decade between 1969 and 1974. In those five years alone, according to the Bureau of Labor Statistics, New York City lost 316,500 jobs. Also, real (after tax) earnings of factory workers in the New York metropolitan area declined 3.7 percent over the 5 years, despite a gain in dollar earnings of 34.5 percent, because of higher taxes and a 39.1 percent jump in living costs. Of the nearly third of a million jobs lost to the city, the largest portion (194,500) were in manufacturing, an industry upon which Puerto Ricans are heavily dependent for employment.[3]

• More and more old factories that employ large numbers of minority workers are shutting down and in some cases relocating at suburban sites. For example, between 1969-74, while New York City lost 316,500 jobs, there was a gain of 211,900 jobs in four suburban counties of New York and eight nearby New Jersey counties.[4] But the same job exodus is occurring in the older cities of New Jersey. Passaic, New Jersey, for example, has a fair-sized Puerto Rican community; in 1973 three large factories ceased operations in Passaic, causing 3,000 employees to seek work elsewhere. In the port city of Hoboken, where Puerto Ricans constitute nearly a third of the population, the rapid growth of container shipment has caused a drop in daily employment for longshoremen from 20,000 to about 12,000 jobs during the past decade. While 77 of the top 250 companies in _Fortune_ magazine's list of 500 were based in New York in 1962, 25 percent of these have since moved out. A report on this massive exodus says:

> A number of companies had moved to the area where many key employees--particularly the chief execu-tive--live. Other considerations that are rarely mentioned, but sometimes considered when a move is made . . . are the number of blacks and Puerto Ricans in the city, crime against persons and property and a dislike of the physical environ-ments.[5]

It is no surprise, then, that between 1950 and 1971, almost all of New York City's job growth was in service-producing industries such as transportation, public utilities, trade, finance, and government.

Looking ahead, the New York State Labor Department projects that between 1968 and 1980 there will be a 12 percent decline in factory jobs and 16 percent for laborers, two areas that have heavy concentrations of Puerto Rican workers.

A U.S. Labor Department study[6] predicts that between 1968 and 1980, the largest number of job openings in New York City will occur in the following areas:

Stenographers, typists, secretaries	144,000
Hospital attendants	36,000
Nurses	35,000
Office machine operators	33,000
Accountants, auditors	26,000
Medical and dental technicians	22,000
Cashiers	22,000
Counter fountain workers	21,000
Elementary schoolteachers	21,000
Private household workers	19,000

In percentage terms, the fastest-growing occupations will be:

Medical and dental technicians	83
Programmers and systems analysts	62
Hospital attendants	49
Social scientists	43
Practical nurses	40
Office machine operators	37
Registered nurses	37

As can be seen from these two projections, job opportunities will be best for: (1) women; (2) persons with very specialized training; and (3) those prepared to do very menial labor at relatively low salaries. This is a far cry from the time early in this century when a man could take root in America and support his family on the basis of his brawn and determination. One suspects that job opportunities have a similar pattern in other eastern cities. Thus, unless there is radical improvement in the education and training of Puerto Ricans, unless there is migration to areas where jobs exist, unless the American economy heats up and provides jobs for the many poor, semiskilled or unskilled persons who are now marginal to the society, unless the federal government finally delivers the guaranteed family income plan that has so long been debated, it appears that Puerto Ricans and all groups who now inhabit the inner cities will face a grim struggle for economic survival in the coming decade.

NOTES

1. New York *Times*, February 2, 1974, p. 10; excerpts from the President's Annual Economic Report of 1974.
2. New York *Times*, October 15, 1972, p. 58.
3. Ibid., September 11, 1974, p. 23.
4. Ibid.
5. Ibid., September 21, 1972.
6. U.S. Department of Labor, Bureau of Labor Statistics, Middle Atlantic Regional Office, New York, *The Economics of Working and Living in New York City*, Regional Report No. 29, July 1972, 64 pp.

TABLE 1

Growth of Puerto Rican Population in the United States, 1910-70

Year	Total	Percent of In- crease	Percent of Total in New York City	Born in Puerto Rico	Born in United States
1910	1,513	--	36.6	1,513	--
1920	11,811	680.6	62.3	11,811	--
1930	52,774	346.8	--	52,774	--
1940	69,967	32.6	87.8	69,967	--
1950	301,375	330.7	81.6	226,110	75,265
1960	887,662	194.5	69.0	615,384	272,278
1970	1,429,396	61.0	56.8	783,358	646,038

Note: Census reports do not list Puerto Ricans born in the United States between 1910 and 1940. Therefore, the total of those "born in Puerto Rico" is given in this table as the complete total. Third-generation Puerto Ricans--children of parents born in the United States--are apparently not included in these tables, since the census takers usually count only those persons born in Puerto Rico, or persons of Puerto Rican parentage.

Sources: 1960 data based on 1960 U.S. Census, "Puerto Ricans in the United States," PC(2)1D, Table A, p. viii; 1970 data from 1970 U.S. Census, "Persons of Spanish Ancestry," PC(SI)-30, February 1973, Table I, p. 1.

TABLE 2

Puerto Rican Populations in the United States and Puerto Rico, 1960 and 1970

Populations	1960	1970
In Puerto Rico	2,349,540	2,712,033
Born in Puerto Rico	2,287,200	2,432,828
Born in United States to Puerto Rican parents	49,092	106,602
On the U.S. mainland	887,662	1,429,396
Born in Puerto Rico	615,384	783,358
Born in United States to Puerto Rican parents	272,278	646,038

Note: Census figures for Puerto Ricans on the U.S. mainland have been challenged as being too low. The Census Bureau itself asserts that there has been an undercount.

Source: 1970 U.S. Census, "Puerto Ricans in the United States," PC(2)1E, Table 1, p. xi.

TABLE 3

Ethnic Intermarriage of Puerto Ricans in the United
States, 1970

	All Puerto Ricans	Born in Puerto Rico	Born in United States
Married males, spouse present	239,131	214,051	25,080
Above, with Puerto Rican spouse	190,142	176,967	13,175
Percent with Puerto Rican spouse	79.5	82.7	52.5
Married females, spouse present	233,962	205,977	27,985
Above, with Puerto Rican spouse	188,836	173,363	15,473
Percent with Puerto Rican spouse	80.7	84.2	55.3

Source: 1970 U.S. Census, PC(2)-1E, Table 5, p. 39.

TABLE 4

Relative Size of Spanish Origin Ethnic Groups in the
United States, 1972
(numbers in thousands)

Origin	Total	Percent Distribution
All persons in United States	204,840	100.0
Persons of Spanish origin	9,178	4.5
Mexican	5,254	2.6
Puerto Rican	1,518	0.7
Cuban	629	0.3
Central or South American	599	0.3
Other Spanish	1,178	0.5
Persons not of Spanish origin	195,662	95.5

Source: U.S. Census Bureau, Current Population Reports, "Population Characteristics," Series P-20, No. 238,
July 1972, p. 3. Figures for March 1972.

TABLE 5

States of Residence of Puerto Ricans on the U.S. Mainland, 1960-70

State	1960	1970
Alabama	663	1,028
Alaska	562	534
Arizona	1,008	1,047
Arkansas	207	139
California	28,108	50,917
Colorado	844	1,707
Connecticut	15,247	37,609
Delaware	773	2,486
District of Columbia	1,373	1,046
Florida	19,535	28,166
Georgia	2,334	3,615
Hawaii	4,289	9,300
Idaho	60	232
Illinois	36,081	87,509
Indiana	7,218	9,269
Iowa	226	428
Kansas	1,136	683
Kentucky	1,376	860
Louisiana	1,935	2,430
Maine	403	426
Maryland	3,229	6,262
Massachusetts	5,217	23,332
Michigan	3,806	6,202
Minnesota	387	490
Mississippi	301	478
Missouri	940	1,801
Montana	53	341
Nebraska	333	389
Nevada	179	674
New Hampshire	212	425
New Jersey	55,351	138,896
New Mexico	433	411
New York	642,622	916,825
North Carolina	1,866	2,482
North Dakota	68	88
Ohio	13,940	20,272
Oklahoma	1,398	1,124
Oregon	233	522
Pennsylvania	21,206	44,263
Rhode Island	447	981
South Carolina	1,114	2,096
South Dakota	124	44
Tennessee	499	1,127
Texas	6,050	6,334
Utah	473	739
Vermont	108	215
Virginia	2,971	4,098
Washington	1,739	1,845
West Virginia	252	73
Wisconsin	3,574	7,248
Wyoming	50	56

Sources: 1960 U.S. Census, "Puerto Ricans in the United States," PC(2)1D, Table 15, pp. 103-04; 1970 U.S. Census, Supplementary Report, "Persons of Spanish Ancestry," PC(SI)-30, February 1973, Table I, p. 1.

TABLE 6

U.S. Cities and Places with 5,000 or More Puerto Ricans,
1960-70

City or Place	1960	1970
New York, N.Y. (city)	612,574	846,731
New York City (urban balance)	--	40,388
Chicago, Ill. (city)	32,371	78,826
Chicago (urban balance)	--	7,451
Newark, N.J. (city)	9,698	26,394
Newark (urban balance)	--	10,615
Philadelphia, Pa. (city)	14,424	26,367
Philadelphia (urban balance)	--	14,563
Jersey City, N.J. (city)	7,427	19,362
Paterson, N.J. (city)	5,123	13,378
Los Angeles, Calif. (city)	6,424	10,294
Los Angeles-Long Beach (urban balance)	--	10,206
Hoboken, N.J. (city)	5,313	10,047
Bridgeport, Conn. (city)	5,840	9,618
Hartford, Conn. (city)	--	8,278
Cleveland, Ohio (city)	--	8,135
Boston, Mass. (city)	--	7,747
Washington, D.C. (city and urban balance)	--	6,732
Passaic, N.J. (city)	--	6,609
Miami, Fla. (city)	6,547	6,446
Miami (urban balance)	--	12,472
Honolulu, Hawaii (city and urban balance)	--	6,428
Buffalo, N.Y. (city and urban balance)	--	6,090
Rochester, N.Y. (city)	--	5,916
Milwaukee, Wis. (city	--	5,889
Lorain, Ohio (city and urban balance)	--	5,601
Gary, Ind. (city)	--	5,228
San Francisco, Calif. (city)	--	5,037
San Francisco-Oakland (urban balance)	--	8,474

Sources: 1960 U.S. Census, "Puerto Ricans in the
United States," PC(2) 1D, Table 15, p. 103; 1970 U.S. Census, "Persons of Spanish Ancestry," PC(SI)-30, February
1973, Table 2, pp. 2-8.

TABLE 7

Age Distribution of Total U.S. Population, Persons of Spanish Origin, Mexicans, Puerto Ricans, and Cubans, 1972
(numbers in thousands)

Age	Total Population	Spanish Origin			
		Total*	Mexican	Puerto Rican	Cuban
Under 5 years old	8.5	12.7	13.4	14.0	4.9
5 to 9 years old	9.2	13.8	15.0	14.7	11.6
10 to 17 years old	16.0	19.4	20.2	21.5	13.4
18 and 19 years old	3.6	3.8	4.3	2.6	3.8
20 to 24 years old	8.4	7.8	8.3	8.0	3.7
25 to 34 years old	12.9	14.2	13.3	14.8	13.8
35 to 44 years old	11.0	11.8	10.8	12.6	15.4
45 to 54 years old	11.4	8.0	7.5	5.3	14.5
55 to 64 years old	9.2	5.0	3.9	4.6	12.1
65 years old and over	9.7	3.5	3.2	2.0	3.8
Median age (years)	28.0	20.1	18.6	17.9	34.1
Total	204,840	9,178	5,254	1,518	629
Percent	100.0	100.0	100.0	100.0	100.0

*Includes other persons of Spanish origin, not shown separately.

Source: U.S. Census Bureau, "Population Characteristics," Series P-20, No. 238, July 1972, p. 3. Figures for March 1972.

TABLE 8

Family Characteristics of Total U.S. Population, Persons of Spanish Origin, Mexicans, and Puerto Ricans, 1972

(numbers in thousands)

Subject	Total Population	Spanish Origin		
		Total*	Mexican	Puerto Rican
Head of family	28.3	24.9	22.7	26.3
Male	25.0	20.6	19.5	18.7
Female	3.3	4.3	3.2	7.6
Wife of head	24.3	15.7	15.7	13.8
Child of head	42.4	53.1	55.3	55.0
Other relative	5.0	6.3	6.2	4.9
Total families	53,296	2,057	1,100	363
No own children under 18	44.8	27.4	23.0	24.2
With own children under 18	55.2	72.6	77.0	75.8
1 own child	18.9	19.8	19.8	19.2
2 own children	17.6	20.9	21.3	22.7
3 own children	10.2	12.9	12.5	13.9
4 own children	4.9	9.5	10.7	10.1
5 own children	2.1	4.9	6.9	4.8
6 or more own children	1.6	4.6	5.9	5.0
Average number of own children under 18 per family	1.22	1.89	2.11	1.97
Percent of families with female head	11.6	17.3	14.1	28.9
Average population per family	3.5	4.0	4.4	3.8
Total family members	188,243	8,277	4,841	1,381
Percent	100.0	100.0	100.0	100.0

*Includes other persons of Spanish origin, not shown separately.

Source: U.S. Census Bureau, "Population Characteristics," Series P-20, No. 238, July 1972, p. 4. Figures for March 1972.

TABLE 9

Family Size and Fertility Data for Puerto Ricans in the United States, 1960 and 1970

	1960			1970		
	All	Born in Puerto Rico	Born in United States	All	Born in Puerto Rico	Born in United States
Family heads	219,495	204,935	14,560	326,460	293,774	32,686
Percent female heads	13.6	13.8	11.6	24.1	24.4	21.0
Percent families with children under 18	--	--	--	75.3	75.1	76.4
Children for 1,000 married women:						
Ages 15 to 24	--	--	--	1,427	1,507	1,074
Ages 25 to 34	--	--	--	2,750	2,812	2,272
Ages 35 to 44	--	--	--	3,503	3,563	3,007
Average persons per family	3.95	--	--	4.15	4.18	3.85

Sources: 1960 U.S. Census, "Puerto Ricans in the United States," PC(2)1D, Table 2, pp. 12, 14, 16; 1970 U.S. Census, "Puerto Ricans in the United States," PC(2)-1E, Table 4, p. 34.

77

TABLE 10

Passenger Traffic to and from Puerto Rico for Fiscal Years
1940-73

Fiscal Year	Departures and Arrivals	Net Balance
1940	48,856	-1,008
1941	61,332	-500
1942	58,032	-928
1943	36,133	-2,601
1944	47,084	-8,088
1945	56,477	-11,003
1946	116,615	-24,621
1947	237,374	-35,144
1948	237,015	-28,031
1949	281,590	-33,086
1950	307,299	-34,155
1951	335,876	-41,920
1952	456,110	-61,658
1953	535,217	-74,603
1954	561,805	-44,209
1955	599,800	-31,182
1956	700,253	-61,647
1957	831,028	-48,284
1958	910,018	-25,956
1959	1,078,190	-37,212
1960	1,309,770	-23,742
1961	1,350,164	-13,800
1962	1,603,735	-11,363
1963	1,856,534	-4,798
1964	2,148,440	-4,366
1965	2,519,434	-10,758
1966	2,920,367	-30,089
1967	3,223,644	-34,174
1968	3,697,621	-18,681
1969	4,217,481	-7,047
1970	n.a.	-20,715
1971	n.a.	-4,951
1972	n.a.	-34,015
1973	n.a.	-20,948

Note: Balance over 30 years (between 1940 and 1969) is a
migration from Puerto Rico of 750,650, which closely corresponds
to the 1970 figure of 783,358 island-born Puerto Ricans in the
United States. The average outflow from the island per year
since 1940 is 25,018.

Source: Puerto Rico Planning Board, except for years 1970-
73, figures for which were supplied by the commonwealth of Puerto
Rico office in New York, and were labeled as "unofficial."

TABLE 11

Children Born to U.S. Women and Puerto Rican Women in the
United States, 1970

| | | Puerto Rican Women in United States | |
	All U.S. Women	Born in Puerto Rico	Born in United States
Women ages 15 to 24			
Ever married	6,453,186	53,006	12,053
Children per 1,000 women ever married	995	1,507	1,074
Women ages 25 to 34			
Ever married	11,416,701	93,998	12,033
Children per 1,000 women ever married	2,374	2,812	2,272
Women ages 35 to 44			
Ever married	11,197,317	71,335	8,617
Children per 1,000 women ever married	3,132	3,563	3,007

Sources: Figures for all U.S. women from 1970 U.S.
Census, "United States Summary," PC(1)-C1, Table 76, pp.
1-369; for Puerto Rican women in the United States from
1970 U.S. Census, "Puerto Ricans in the United States,"
PC(2)-1E, Table 4, p. 34.

TABLE 12

Puerto Ricans in Puerto Rico, by Birthplace and Residence,
1960-70

	1960	1970
Total population	2,349,540	2,712,033
Born in Puerto Rico	2,287,200	2,432,828
Born in the United States to		
Puerto Rican parents	49,092	106,602
Percent	2.1	4.0
Residence five years previous	55,648	129,105
Percent	2.8	5.4

Source: 1970 U.S. Census, "Puerto Rico," PC(1)-C53
P.R., Table 38, pp. 53-187.

TABLE 13

Population of Whites, Blacks, and Puerto Ricans in the
United States, Ages 25 and Above, with Less Than Five
Years of School or with Four Years of High School, 1971
(in percent)

	Less Than Five Years of School	High School Graduates
Whites	4.1	58.6
Blacks	13.5	34.7
Puerto Ricans	23.7	19.8
Total U.S.	5.0	56.4

Source: U.S. Census Bureau, "Selected Characteristics of Persons and Families of Mexican, Puerto Rican and Other Spanish Origin: March 1971," Series P-20, No. 224, October 1971, Table 10, p. 12.

TABLE 14

Education: Percent of the Population 25 Years Old and Over Who Had Completed Less Than Five Years of School or Four Years of High School or More, for Total U.S. Population, Persons of Spanish Origin, Mexicans, and Puerto Ricans, 1972

Years of School Completed and Age	Total Population	Spanish Origin		
		Total*	Mexican	Puerto Rican
Completed Less Than Five Years of School				
Total 25 years old and over	4.6	19.3	26.7	20.2
25 to 29 years old	0.8	5.5	7.3	5.8
30 to 34 years old	1.4	8.4	12.6	8.7
35 to 44 years old	2.5	15.9	21.0	19.9
45 to 54 years old	3.4	25.1	33.1	39.9
55 to 64 years old	5.6	30.8	47.9	(B)
65 years old and over	12.2	51.3	74.8	(B)
Completed Four Years of High School or More				
Total 25 years old and over	58.2	33.0	25.8	23.7
25 to 29 years old	79.8	47.6	42.9	30.9
30 to 34 years old	73.9	42.7	40.1	22.6
35 to 44 years old	66.8	35.2	28.0	27.2
45 to 54 years old	59.8	24.9	14.2	21.3
55 to 64 years old	46.7	20.6	8.8	(B)
65 years old and over	32.0	12.1	0.6	(B)

*Includes other persons of Spanish origin.

B = Base less than 75,000

Source: U.S. Census Bureau, Current Population Reports, Series P-20, No. 238, July 1972, p. 5. Data for March 1972.

TABLE 15

Educational Attainment for Puerto Ricans in the United States, 25 Years Old and Over, 1971

	Persons 25 to 34 Years Old		Persons 35 Years and Older	
	Number	Percent	Number	Percent
Elementary school				
0 to 7 years	68,000	31.7	179,000	53.4
8 years	19,000	8.9	54,000	16.1
High school				
1 to 3 years	69,000	32.2	39,000	11.6
4 years	45,000	21.0	45,000	13.4
College				
1 or more years	13,000	6.0	19,000	5.7
Total	214,000		335,000	
Median school years		9.9		7.5

Source: U.S. Census Bureau, "Persons of Spanish Origin in the U.S., November 1969," Series P-20, No. 213, February 1971, Table 14, p. 20.

TABLE 16

Educational Achievements of Puerto Ricans in the United States
and in Puerto Rico, and the Total U.S. Population, 1970

	All	Puerto Ricans in the United States Born in Puerto Rico	Born in United States	Puerto Ricans in Puerto Rico	Total U.S. Population
Population age 25 or above	567,462	509,456	58,006	1,196,692	109,899,359
Percent with less than five years of schools	23.7			37.8	5.0
Percent with four years high school	23.0	20.5	45.6	27.0	52.3
Percent with four years college	2.2	1.9	5.4	6.0	10.0
Median school years completed	8.6	8.4	11.5	6.9	12.1

Sources: 1970 U.S. Census, "Puerto Ricans in the United States," PC(2)-1E, Table 4, p. 34; 1970 U.S. Census, "General Social and Economic Characteristics, Puerto Rico," PC(1) 53 P.R., Table 45, pp. 53-197; 1970 U.S. Census, "General Social and Economic Characteristics, United States Summary," PC(1)-C1, Table 75, pp. 1-368.

TABLE 17

Median School Years Completed, for Puerto Ricans in the United
States and in Puerto Rico, 1950, 1960, and 1970

	All	Puerto Ricans in the United States Born in Puerto Rico	Born in United States	Puerto Ricans in Puerto Rico
1950				
Males 25 years and over	8.2	8.0	9.8	4.1
Females 25 years and over	8.0	7.5	10.1	3.3
1960				
Males 14 years and over	8.4	8.2	10.3	6.1
Females 14 years and over	8.2	8.0	10.8	5.6
1970				
Males and females 25 years and over	8.6	8.4	11.5	6.9

Sources: 1950 U.S. Census Report, P-E 3D, Table 4, pp. 3D-13; 1960 U.S. Census Report, PC(51)-34, Table 42, p. 9; 1960 U.S. Census Report, PC(2)1D, Table 2, pp. 12, 14, 16; 1970 U.S. Census Report, PC(2)1E, Table 4, p. 34; 1970 U.S. Census Report, PC(1)D53 P.R., Table 80, p. 249.

TABLE 18

School Enrollment of Puerto Ricans in the United States, by Age Group and Place of Birth, 1960-70

	1960			1970		
	Total	P.R.-born	U.S.-born	Total	P.R.-born	U.S.-born
Percent enrolled in school, ages						
3 to 34 years*	41.7	32.2	68.5	46.8	27.7	67.4
3 and 4 years old	--	--	--	10.6	11.4	10.4
5 and 6 years old	66.4	64.7	67.0	72.4	67.5	73.7
7 to 13 years old	94.9	94.2	95.7	94.9	93.2	95.6
14 to 17 years old						
Males	--	--	--	85.5	78.5	90.7
Females	--	--	--	83.7	75.8	90.0
18 to 24 years old						
Males	--	--	--	18.4	13.3	32.6
Females	--	--	--	14.3	10.3	26.3
25 to 34 years old	3.3	3.1	5.5	2.5	1.9	6.8
Total	223,636	127,488	96,148	437,863	134,501	303,362

*1970 total enrollment percentage is for students ages 3 to 34, while for 1960 it is for ages 5 to 34.

Sources: 1960 U.S. Census, "Puerto Ricans in the United States," PC(2)1D; 1970 U.S. Census, "Puerto Ricans in the United States, PC(2)-1E.

TABLE 19

School Enrollment, by Age Group, in Puerto Rico,
1960 and 1970

Percent Enrolled	1960	1970
5 and 6 years old	29.5	51.4
7 to 13 years old	83.7	91.2
14 and 15 years old	64.7	83.2
16 and 17 years old	47.1	74.2
18 and 19 years old	29.5	56.1
20 and 21 years old	14.8	22.1
22 to 24 years old	8.6	10.7
25 to 34 years old	5.2	6.2
Median school years completed	4.6	6.9

Sources: 1960 U.S. Census, "Puerto Ricans in the
United States," PC(1) 53D P.R., Table 78, p. 241; 1970
U.S. Census, PC(1)-C53 P.R., Table 115, pp. 53-267.

TABLE 20

School Enrollment and Unemployment among Males, Ages 16 to
21, for Puerto Ricans in the United States, for U.S.-born
Puerto Ricans, and for All Males in the U.S. Northeast,
1970

	Puerto Ricans in U.S.	U.S.- born	All Males in U.S. Northeast
Total population	81,056	31,669	2,381,412
Not enrolled in school	44,601	12,408	777,709
Percent	55.0	39.2	32.6
Not enrolled, unemployed	16,022	5,364	129,613
Percent	35.9	43.2	16.6

Sources: 1970 U.S. Census, "United States Summary,"
PC(1)-C1, Table 99, pp. 1-405; 1970 U.S. Census, "Puerto
Ricans in the United States," PC(2)-1E, Table 4, p. 35.

TABLE 21

Mother Tongue of Total U.S. Population, Persons of Spanish Origin, Mexicans, Puerto Ricans, Cubans, Central or South Americans, 1969

	Percent English	Percent Spanish	Other and Not Reported
Total U.S.	81.6	3.4	15.0
Persons of Spanish origin	28.8	68.9	2.3
Mexican	27.0	72.1	0.9
Puerto Rican	15.6	83.1	1.3
Cuban	4.5	94.8	0.7
Central or South American	25.3	68.9	5.6
Other Spanish	56.7	36.2	7.1

Source: U.S. Census Bureau, "Persons of Spanish Origin in the U.S., November 1969," Series P-20, No. 213, February 1971, Table 6, p. 10.

TABLE 22

Language Usually Spoken in the Home, by Total U.S. Population, Persons of Spanish Origin, Mexicans, Puerto Ricans, Cubans, Central or South Americans, 1969

	Percent English	Percent Spanish	Other and Not Reported
Total U.S.	94.1	2.3	3.6
Persons of Spanish origin	50.3	48.7	0.9
Mexican	51.9	47.3	0.8
Puerto Rican	27.0	72.1	0.8
Cuban	12.3	87.0	0.7
Central or South American	42.6	54.2	3.1
Other Spanish	83.0	16.1	0.9

Source: U.S. Census Bureau, "Persons of Spanish Origin in the U.S., November 1969," Series P-20, No. 213, February 1971, Table 10, p. 14.

TABLE 23

Reporting the Ability to Read and Write English, by Total U.S. Population, Persons of Spanish Origin, and Puerto Ricans, 1969

	Puerto Ricans	Persons Spanish Origin	Total U.S. Population
Total age 10 and over	69.4	80.2	95.0
10 to 24 years	80.6	91.1	96.8
25 years or over	59.7	71.9	94.2
Males age 10 and over	72.9	82.8	95.3
10 to 24 years	82.3	91.7	96.7
25 years or over	65.1	75.9	94.6
Females age 10 and over	66.1	77.9	94.8
10 to 24 years	79.1	90.6	96.9
25 years or over	55.6	68.1	93.9

Source: U.S. Census Bureau, "Persons of Spanish Origin in the U.S., November 1969," Series P-20, February 1971, Table 17, p. 23.

TABLE 24

Labor Force Participation, Persons 16 to 64 Years Old, by Age, Sex, and Ethnic Origin for Total U.S.
Population, Persons of Spanish Origin, Mexicans, and Puerto Ricans, March 1972
(numbers in thousands)

Age and Sex	Total Population	Spanish Origin Total*	Mexican	Puerto Rican
Total number male	52,900	2,039	1,175	295
16 to 24 years old	11,938	439	296	60
25 to 44 years old	23,267	1,108	612	182
45 to 64 years old	17,695	492	267	53
Total percent male	86.0	85.0	86.5	76.6
16 to 24 years old	68.2	64.7	70.1	53.1
25 to 44 years old	96.1	95.4	96.5	88.3
45 to 64 years old	88.2	88.0	88.1	(B)
Total number female	31,877	1,055	538	108
16 to 24 years old	8,377	331	217	28
25 to 44 years old	12,593	497	241	58
45 to 64 years old	10,906	227	80	22
Total percent female	49.8	40.2	38.8	26.3
16 to 24 years old	49.9	42.7	47.1	24.3
25 to 44 years old	50.1	40.7	38.3	27.6
45 to 64 years old	49.3	36.1	27.0	25.6

*Includes other persons of Spanish origin.

B = Base less than 75,000

Source: U.S. Census Bureau, Current Population Reports, Series P-20, No. 238, July 1973, p. 6.

TABLE 25

Labor Force Participation by Age of U.S. Males (Whites, Blacks, and Puerto Ricans), 1970

| Age | U.S. Whites | U.S. Blacks | Puerto Ricans in the United States | | |
			All	Born in Puerto Rico	Born in United States
14-15	14.3	8.8	7.2	8.7	6.3
16-17	37.8	22.5	39.2*	44.3*	33.1*
18-19	61.1	51.6	--	--	--
20-24	81.6	75.6	79.6	81.3	73.2
25-34	94.7	87.5	87.2	87.3	87.0
35-44	95.6	88.4	88.2	87.9	90.1
45-64	88.0	80.0	78.2	77.9	82.1
65 plus	24.9	23.7	20.8	20.7	22.3

Note: Figures for Puerto Ricans with asterisk denote from ages 16 to 19.

Sources: 1970 U.S. Census, "United States Summary," PC(1)-C1, Table 78, pp. 1-372; 1970 U.S. Census, "Puerto Ricans in the United States," PC(2)-1E, Table 6, pp. 54, 55.

TABLE 26

Labor Force Participation for U.S. Women, Age 16 and Over, by Number of Children (White, Black, Spanish Heritage, Mexican, Puerto Rican, and Cuban), 1970

	Total	Children Under Age 6	Children Ages 6 to 17	No Children Under 18
White	40.6	28.4	49.0	41.5
Black	47.5	47.6	59.8	43.4
Spanish heritage	38.1	28.4	43.5	41.7
Mexican	37.8	29.8	43.3	40.1
Puerto Rican	29.9	16.6	30.5	39.9
Cuban	47.1	38.6	59.7	45.1

Source: Monthly Labor Review, April 1973, p. 5.

89

TABLE 27

Unemployment Rates for Persons, 16 to 64 Years Old, by Age and Sex (Total U.S.
Population, Spanish Origin, Mexican, and Puerto Rican), 1972

| Age and Sex | Total Population | Total* | Spanish Origin | |
			Mexican	Puerto Rican
Total male	6.0	7.4	7.9	8.8
16 to 24 years old	14.2	16.2	15.1	(B)
25 to 44 years old	4.0	3.9	4.3	6.3
45 to 64 years old	3.6	7.6	8.6	(B)
Total female	6.6	10.0	9.1	17.6
16 to 24 years old	11.9	11.5	12.4	(B)
25 to 44 years old	5.5	9.1	7.1	(B)
45 to 64 years old	3.9	10.1	6.3	(B)

*Includes other persons of Spanish origin.

B = Base less than 75,000.

Source: U.S. Census Bureau, Current Population Reports, Series P-20, No. 238, July
1972, p. 7. Figures for March 1972.

90

TABLE 28

Official and Adjusted Unemployment for Total U.S. Population and Puerto Ricans in the United States, March 1972

(in percent)

Age and Sex	U.S. Total			Puerto Ricans in United States				
	Labor Force Size (number)	Labor Force Participation Rate	Unemployment	Labor Force Size (number)	Labor Force Participation Rate	Official Unemployment	Adjusted Labor Force Size* (number)	Adjusted Unemployment Rate*
Males, ages 16 to 64	52,900,000	86.0	6.0	295,000	76.6	8.8	331,000	18.7
Females, ages 16 to 64	31,877,000	49.8	6.6	108,000	26.3	17.6	204,000	56.4
Males and females, ages 16 to 64	84,777,000	--	6.2	403,000	--	12.6	535,000	33.0

*Adjusted figures for Puerto Ricans are based upon labor force participation rates for the total U.S. population.

Sources: 1970 U.S. Census, "Puerto Ricans in the United States," PC(2)-1E, Table 6, pp. 54, 55; 1970 U.S. Census, "United States Summary," PC(1)-C1, Table 78, pp. 1-372.

TABLE 29

Occupation of Employed Persons by Race, Sex, and Type of Spanish Heritage, April 1970

Occupation Group	Total	White	Black	Spanish Heritage			
				Total	Five South-western States[a]	Three Mid-dle Atlantic States[b]	Florida[c]
Total men (in thousands)	47,624	43,030	4,052	1,897	1,255	194	112
Percent	100.0	100.0	100.0	100.0	100.0	100.0	100.0
Professional, technical and kindred	14.3	15.0	5.8	8.9	8.2	4.0	11.3
Nonfarm managers and administrators	11.2	12.0	3.0	6.3	6.2	4.2	9.0
Sales	6.9	7.4	2.1	4.7	4.5	4.5	7.7
Clerical	7.6	7.6	8.1	7.6	7.0	12.0	8.9
Craftsmen	21.2	21.8	15.2	19.8	20.6	15.4	21.8
Operatives, except transportation	13.6	13.1	19.6	18.7	17.0	25.3	13.5
Transportation equipment operatives	5.9	5.6	10.0	6.5	6.9	7.0	5.2
Nonfarm laborers	6.6	5.7	15.8	10.1	11.2	7.1	6.7
Service, except private household	8.1	7.3	15.6	11.2	10.4	19.4	12.6
Private household	.1	--	.4	.1	.2	.2	.1
Farmworkers	4.5	4.5	4.4	6.2	8.0	.8	3.2
Total women (in thousands)	28,900	25,252	3,309	990	647	91	73
Percent	100.0	100.0	100.0	100.0	100.0	100.0	100.0
Professional, technical and kindred	15.7	16.3	11.3	9.6	9.1	6.5	8.3
Nonfarm managers and administrators	3.6	3.9	1.5	2.4	2.6	1.6	2.2
Sales	7.4	8.1	2.5	6.0	6.3	4.2	6.2
Clerical	34.9	36.9	20.7	30.0	29.9	30.8	28.9
Craftsmen	1.8	1.9	1.4	2.2	2.1	2.4	3.0
Operatives	13.9	13.6	16.1	23.7	20.6	40.3	32.3
Transportation equipment operatives	.5	.5	.4	.4	.4	.3	.4
Nonfarm laborers	1.0	.9	1.5	1.3	1.3	1.1	1.0
Service except private household	16.6	15.4	25.5	18.5	20.1	11.6	14.2
Private household	3.9	2.0	17.9	4.0	5.0	.9	1.9
Farmworkers	.8	.7	1.2	1.9	2.5	.1	1.7

[a] Persons of Spanish language or surname, primarily Mexican Americans.
[b] Persons of Puerto Rican birth or parentage.
[c] Persons of Spanish language, primarily Cubans.

Source: 1970 Census data cited in Monthly Labor Review, April 1973, p. 8.

TABLE 30

Median Family Income and Low-Income Status for All U.S.
Families, Whites, Blacks, Spanish Origin, Mexicans, Puerto
Ricans, and Cubans

	Median Income, 1971		Percentage of Families in 1969 with Incomes Below Low-Income Threshold
	Dollars	Percentage of Whites	
All families	10,285	96	10.7
Whites	10,672	100	8.6
Blacks	6,440	60	29.8
Spanish origin, total	7,548	71	20.4
Mexican	7,486	70	21.2
Puerto Rican	6,185	58	29.0
Cuban	9,371	89	13.8
Other	8,494	80	n.a.

Source: U.S. Census Bureau figures cited in _Monthly Labor Review_, April 1973, Table 1, p. 4.

TABLE 31

Family Income for Total U.S. Population, Spanish Origin, Mexicans, Puerto Ricans, and Cubans

(numbers in thousands)

Total Money Income	Total Population	Spanish Origin Total*	Mexican	Puerto Rican	Cuban
Number of families	53,296	2,057	1,100	363	170
Percent	100.0	100.0	100.0	100.0	100.0
Under $3,000	8.3	13.8	14.9	16.9	7.9
$3,000-3,999	4.8	8.2	9.2	11.0	3.2
$4,000-4,999	5.4	8.4	7.1	10.6	11.3
$5,000-5,999	5.7	8.1	8.3	10.2	8.0
$6,000-6,999	5.5	7.2	7.0	7.7	3.5
$7,000-7,999	6.2	8.0	7.1	12.8	7.6
$8,000-9,999	12.3	13.8	15.1	9.9	11.8
$10,000-11,999	12.5	11.9	11.8	10.6	15.1
$12,000-14,999	14.4	10.4	10.2	5.1	10.2
$15,000-24,999	19.5	9.5	8.6	4.5	20.6
$25,000 and over	5.3	0.9	0.5	0.8	0.8
Median income (dollars)	10,285	7,548	7,486	6,185	9,371
Head year-round, full-time worker:					
Median family income (dollars)	12,436	9,596	9,472	8,235	11,296
Percent of all families	63.5	57.0	57.5	50.7	61.8

*Includes other persons of Spanish origin.

Source: U.S. Census Bureau, Current Population Reports, Series P-20, No. 238, July 1972, p. 8. Income figures for 1971; family figures as of March 1972.

TABLE 32

Median Income of Puerto Ricans in the United States, Age
14 and Over, by Years of School Completed, 1970
(in dollars)

Total	3,910
Elementary school	
0 to 4 years	3,000
5 to 7 years	3,800
8 years	4,167
High school	
1 to 3 years	4,056
4 years	5,222

Source: U.S. Census Bureau, "Persons of Spanish
Origin in the U.S., March 1972 and 1971," Series P-20, No.
250, April 1973, Table A-14, p. 34.

TABLE 33

Income Levels of Puerto Rican Families with Persons 3-18
Years Old in Households, by Mother Tongue, 1969

	English	Spanish
Percent by income	100.0	100.0
Under $3,000	7.7	17.1
Under $1,000	1.2	1.9
$1,000-1,999	2.5	6.0
$2,000-2,999	4.0	9.2
$3,000-3,999	5.5	12.7
$4,000-5,999	13.9	29.6
$6,000-9,999	32.8	24.9
$10,000 or more	34.5	7.8
Not reported	5.7	7.9

Source: U.S. Census Bureau, "Persons of Spanish
Origin in the U.S., November 1969," Series P-20, No. 213,
February 1971, Table 27, p. 35.

TABLE 34

Median Family Income for U.S. Population, Whites, Blacks, and Puerto Ricans in United States and in Puerto Rico, 1959, 1970, 1971
(in dollars)

	1959	Percentage of Whites	1970	Percentage of Whites	1971	Percentage of Whites
U.S. population	5,660	96.0	9,867	96.4	10,285	96.4
Whites	5,893	100.0	10,236	100.0	10,672	100.0
Blacks	3,161	53.6	6,279	61.3	6,440	60.3
Puerto Ricans	3,811	64.6	5,975	58.3	6,185	57.9
In Puerto Rico	1,268	21.5	3,063	29.9	--	--

Sources: 1959 and 1969 figures from 1970 U.S. Census, "United States Summary," PC(1)-C1, Table 83, p. 1-377, except for Puerto Rican data, which comes from 1960 U.S. Census, "Puerto Ricans in the United States," PC(2)1D, Table 14, p. 102; 1970 figures from U.S. Census Current Population Reports, Series P-20, No. 224, October 1971, Table 3, p. 5; 1971 figures from U.S. Census, Current Population Reports, Series P-20, No. 238, July 1972, Table 9, p. 8.

TABLE 35

Low-Income Status of Persons in the United States (Total
U.S., Persons of Spanish Origin, Mexicans, Puerto Ricans,
and Cubans), 1971
(numbers in thousands)

| Origin | Total | Below-Low-Income Level | |
		Number	Percent
All persons, U.S.	204,554	25,559	12.5
Persons of Spanish origin	9,178	2,350	25.6
Mexican	5,254	1,520	28.9
Puerto Rican*	1,518	489	32.2
Cuban	629	74	11.8
Other	1,777	266	15.0
Persons not of Spanish origin	195,376	23,209	11.9

*In 1970, 29.2 percent of Puerto Rican families were
beneath the poverty level, compared with 59.6 percent of
the families on the island of Puerto Rico.

Source: U.S. Census Bureau, Current Population Reports, Series P-20, No. 238, July 1972, p. 9. Data taken
in March 1972, for income in 1972.

97

TABLE 36

Housing Data for Total United States and for U.S. Puerto
Ricans by Birthplace, 1970

| | | U.S. Puerto Ricans | | |
	Nationwide	All	Head Born in Puerto Rico	Head Born in United States
Households	54,159,018	365,227	327,261	37,996
Percent in owner-occupied units	59.1	14.8	13.9	22.4
Percent of structures built before 1939	--	65.9	67.5	51.9
Percent of structures built 1969 to March 1970	--	0.9	0.8	1.9
Percent without autos	--	63.7	65.4	49.5
Value of owner-occupied units (dollars)	20,771*	18,200	17,300	22,300
Rent paid (dollars)	121*	83	83	90

*Figures with asterisk represent nationwide figures for urban
areas, since, for sake of accurate comparison, most Puerto Rican
families live in urban areas.

Sources: 1970 U.S. Census, "United States Summary," PC(1)-
C1, Table 117, pp. 1-423; 1970 U.S. Census, "Puerto Ricans in the
United States," PC(2)-1E, Table 10, p. 94.

TABLE 37

Poverty and Welfare in the United States (Whites, Blacks, and
U.S. Puerto Ricans by Birthplace), 1970

| | | | U.S. Puerto Ricans | | |
	Whites	Blacks	All	Born in Puerto Rico	Born in United States
Percent of families that receive public assistance income	4.0	17.6	24.5	25.1	18.6
Percent of families under poverty level	8.6	29.8	27.1	27.8	20.1

Sources: 1970 U.S. Census, "United States Summary," PC(1)-
C1, Table 117, pp. 1-423 and Table 123, pp. 1-435; 1970 U.S. Census, "Puerto Ricans in the United States," PC(2)-1E, Table 9, p.
89.

TABLE 38

General Social and Economic Characteristics of White, Black, and
Puerto Rican Persons in New York State, 1970

	White	Black	Puerto Rican
Population	15,885,867	2,164,560	872,471
Percent of total	86.8	11.9	4.8
Median age	31.5	24.8	20.9
Percent enrolled in school, ages 3 to 34	55.4	50.5	46.8
Percent of population enrolled in college	3.8	1.8	1.0
Median school years, males age 25 and over	12.2	10.8	8.8
Median school years, females age 25 and over	12.1	10.9	8.3
Percent high school graduates, age 25 and over	54.2	39.8	20.9
Percent college graduates, age 25 and over	12.7	4.2	1.2
Percent disabled or handicapped, ages 16 to 64	9.2	13.0	12.1
Percent veterans of armed forces, males age 16 and over	42.9	35.0	23.2
Percent males, age 16 and over in labor force	76.3	70.9	71.6
Percent unemployed	3.4	5.6	6.1
Percent females, age 16 and over in labor force	40.5	47.3	28.8
Percent unemployed	4.5	5.2	7.8
Number of persons employed, age 16 and over	6,289,241	758,488	233,090
Percent of population that is employed	39.6	35.0	26.7
Percent of employed in professional-technical jobs	17.5	9.8	4.8
Percent share of teaching jobs	95.1	4.4	0.5
Number of families	4,069,135	497,950	212,922
Median family income (dollars)	11,034	7,297	5,698
Percent families earning:			
$15,000-25,000 a year	20.9	9.7	4.4
$25,000-50,000 a year	6.1	1.3	0.5
$50,000 plus a year	1.4	0.2	0.1
Percent families below poverty level	7.0	20.1	29.6
Percent families that receive public assistance	4.6	20.1	28.8

Source: 1970 U.S. Census, "General Social and Economic
Characteristics, New York," PC(1)-C34 N.Y., Tables 45-58.

TABLE 39

General Social and Economic Characteristics for Puerto Ricans in New York State Counties with 5,000 or More Puerto Ricans, 1970

County	Population	Median Age	School Years, Male Adults	Median Family Income (in dollars)	Percent Families in Poverty
Bronx	316,772	21.1	9.0	5,578	30.4
Erie	5,167	15.2	7.0	6,459	33.1
Kings	271,769	18.8	8.6	5,251	34.5
Monroe	5,792	16.5	8.2	7,689	15.8
Nassau	7,224	23.1	10.7	10,534	10.2
New York	185,323	23.5	8.7	5,543	28.2
Queens	33,141	25.5	10.2	8,870	10.8
Suffolk	17,179	20.4	10.5	10,085	11.3
Westchester	5,715	19.5	9.7	7,889	22.1

Source: 1970 U.S. Census, "General Social and Economic Characteristics, New York," PC(1)-C34 N.Y., Tables 129-133.

TABLE 40

Place of Residence of Puerto Ricans in New York State,
1970

Areas and places with 50,000 or more total population:	
Albany	155
Binghamton	56
Buffalo	3,880
Levittown	541
Mt. Vernon	316
Rochester	5,456
Syracuse	757
New Rochelle	258
Niagara Falls	69
Schenectady	181
Troy	114
Utica	468
Rome	108
White Plains	343
Yonkers	2,630
New York City	811,843
Places of 10,000 to 50,000 total population with 400 or more Puerto Ricans:	
Beacon	617
Brentwood	1,600
Central Islip	1,666
Deer Park	435
Dunkirk	678
Geneva	404
Glen Cove	589
Huntington Station	455
Lackawanna	657
Long Beach	661
Middletown	527
Newburgh	1,147
North Great River	871
Patchogue	904
Peekskill	579
Wyandanch	531

Source: 1970 U.S. Census, "General Social and Economic Characteristics, New York," PC(1)-034. N.Y., Tables 96-101 and 112-16.

TABLE 41

General Social and Economic Characteristics of Total, Black, and Puerto
Rican Populations, New York City SMSA, 1970

	Total	Black	Puerto Rican
Population	11,571,819	1,822,848	845,775
Percent share	100.0	16.7	7.3
Education			
School enrollment, ages 3 to 34	3,041,022	550,515	261,956
Percent enrolled, ages 3 to 34	53.1	50.0	46.8
Median school years, males age 25 and over	12.1	10.9	8.9
Median school years, females age 25 and over	12.0	10.9	8.3
High school enrollment	754,214	132,585	58,165
Percent share	100.0	17.5	7.7
College enrollment	396,491	33,759	8,602
Percent share	100.0	8.5	2.2
Employment			
Males, age 16 and over	3,863,065	529,724	227,793
Percent in labor force	75.8	71.8	72.0
Percent unemployed	3.5	5.2	6.1
Females, age 16 and over	4,537,158	697,744	275,240
Percent in labor force	41.5	47.1	28.5
Percent unemployed	4.3	4.8	7.7
Total persons employed, age 16 and over	4,607,100	671,665	225,869
Professional-technical workers	777,843	66,600	10,805
Percent share	100.0	8.6	1.4
Doctors and dentists	48,627	1,377	234
Percent share	100.0	2.7	0.5
Teachers	150,909	9,354	1,145
Percent share	100.0	6.1	0.7
Managers-administrators	419,549	21,284	8,150
Percent share	100.0	5.0	1.9
Factory operatives	455,439	87,047	60,883
Percent share	100.0	19.0	13.4
Income			
Number of families	2,970,425	440,232	207,868
Median family income (dollars)	10,870	7,313	5,666
Percent families that earn under $1,000	2.8	6.0	7.9
Percent families that earn over $15,000	29.2	11.5	4.9
Per capita income (dollars)	3,922	2,411	1,765
Percent families below poverty level	7.6	20.1	29.1
Percent families on public assistance	9.2	19.9	29.8

Note: The New York City Standard Metropolitan Statistical Area (SMSA)
includes New York City with a Puerto Rican population of 811,843, Levittown (541), Mount Vernon (316), New Rochelle (258), White Plains (343),
Yonkers (2,630), and the surrounding urban balance (29,024).

Source: 1970 U.S. Census, "General Social and Economic Characteristics, New York," PC(1)-C34 N.Y., Tables 31-90, 91-95, and 96-101.

TABLE 42

Racial and Ethnic Change in New York City Population,
1950, 1960, and 1970
(numbers in thousands)

| Ethnic Group | 1950 | 1960 | 1970 | Percent Change | |
				1950-60	1960-70
Total	7,892	7,782	7,896	-1.4	1.5
White[a]	7,116	6,641	6,049	-6.7	-8.9
Black and other races[a]	776	1,141	1,847	47.0	61.9
Puerto Rican[b]	246	613	812	149.2	32.5

[a]Includes Puerto Ricans.
[b]1970 total for Puerto Ricans is a preliminary estimate by the
U.S. Census Bureau, and has been challenged.

Source: 1970 U.S. Census, "Puerto Ricans in the United
States," PC(2)-1E, Table 1, p. xi.

TABLE 43

Estimated Annual Cost of Family Consumption for Selected Family
Types, New York-Northeastern New Jersey, Autumn 1971
(in dollars)

Family Size, Type, Age	Lower Level	Inter-mediate Level	Higher Level
Single persons, under 35 years	2,136	3,422	4,880
Husband and wife under 35:			
No children	2,991	4,791	6,832
1 child under 6	3,784	6,062	8,645
2 children, eldest under 6	4,395	7,039	10,039
Husband and wife, ages 35 to 54:			
1 child, ages 6 to 15	5,005	8,017	11,433
2 children, eldest ages 6 to 15	6,104	9,777	13,943
3 children, eldest ages 6 to 15	7,081	11,341	16,174
Single persons, 65 years and older	1,709	2,738	3,904
Husband and wife, 65 years and over	3,113	4,986	7,111

Source: U.S. Department of Labor, Bureau of Labor Statistics, Middle Atlantic Regional Office, New York, "The Economics
of Working and Living in New York City," Regional Report No. 29,
July 1972, Table 11, p. 24.

TABLE 44

New York City Population by Borough and Ethnic Group, 1970
(in thousands)

| | 1970 Census | | 1970 Population Health Survey | |
	People	Percent	People	Percent
New York City	7,894.9	100.0	7,875.0	100.0
White	5,237.0	66.3	5,082.5	64.5
Black	1,846.0	23.4	1,776.0	22.5
Puerto Rican	811.8	10.3	1,016.5	12.9
Manhattan	1,539.2	100.0	1,683.0	100.0
White	904.0	58.7	912.0	54.2
Black	449.9	29.2	480.5	28.5
Puerto Rican	185.3	12.0	290.5	17.3
Bronx	1,471.7	100.0	1,444.5	100.0
White	764.1	51.9	691.5	47.9
Black	390.8	26.5	378.0	26.2
Puerto Rican	316.8	21.5	375.0	25.9
Brooklyn	2,602.0	100.0	2,578.5	100.0
White	1,634.0	62.8	1,588.5	61.6
Black	696.2	26.7	680.0	26.4
Puerto Rican	271.8	10.4	310.0	12.0
Queens	1,986.5	100.0	1,895.0	100.0
White	1,662.2	83.7	1,634.5	86.2
Black	291.2	14.6	228.0	12.0
Puerto Rican	33.1	1.7	*	*
Richmond	295.4	100.0	274.0	100.0
White	272.8	92.3	256.0	93.4
Black	17.8	6.0	*	*
Puerto Rican	4.8	1.6	*	*

*Insufficient data.

Source: Morey J. Wantman et al., "Estimates of Population Characteristics New York City, 1964-65-66-68-70," Population Health Survey Research Bulletin, Center for Social Research, City University of New York, RB-P14-72, December 1972, Table IV, p. 8.

TABLE 45

Racial and Ethnic Distribution of Students in New York
City's Public Schools, 1970

	Pupils	Percent of Total
Puerto Rican	260,040	22.8
Other Spanish-surname Americans	39,240	3.4
Black	392,714	34.4
American Indian	349	--
Oriental	17,491	1.6
Other	431,241	37.8

Source: Board of Education of the City of New York,
Office of Business Administration, "Annual Census of
School Population, October 30, 1970, Summary Tables," Pub-
lication No. 340, P.N. S 411, April 1971, Table I.

TABLE 46

Ethnic Composition of New York City's Public Schools,
as of October 1960, 1965, and 1970

	1960	1965	1970
Puerto Rican			
Number	153,697	211,706	260,040
Percent	15.6	19.8	22.8
Black			
Number	212.006	302,287	392,714
Percent	21.5	28.4	34.4
Other			
Number	620,976	551,927	488,321
Percent	62.9	51.8	42.8

*"Other" refers primarily to white, North American
students, but also includes other Spanish-surnamed Americans, Orientals, and American Indians.

Source: Board of Education of the City of New York,
Office of Business Administration, "Annual Census of
School Population, October 30, 1970, Summary Tables," Pub-
lication No. 340, P.N. S 411, April 1971, Chart iv.

TABLE 47

Distribution of Puerto Rican Students in New York City
Public Schools, by Borough and School Level, 1970

	Puerto Rican Students	Percent of All Students
Manhattan		
Elementary	31,873	34.4
Junior high-intermediate	11,671	34.2
Academic high	10,963	29.7
Vocational high	3,704	32.2
Bronx		
Elementary	59,957	42.8
Junior high-intermediate	19,060	38.9
Academic high	12,215	28.6
Vocational high	3,301	53.3
Brooklyn		
Elementary	57,894	25.4
Junior high-intermediate	20,151	22.8
Academic high	11,462	13.0
Vocational high	4,665	33.4
Queens		
Elementary	4,388	3.4
Junior high-intermediate	1,831	3.6
Academic high	2,222	3.4
Vocational high	994	15.4
Richmond		
Elementary	805	3.0
Junior high-intermediate	264	2.6
Academic high	305	2.4
Vocational high	53	5.6

Source: Board of Education of the City of New York,
Office of Business Administration, "Annual Census of
School Population, October 30, 1970, Summary Tables," Pub-
lication No. 340, P.N. S 411, April 1971, Table iii.
Totals do not include pupils enrolled in "Special Schools,"
which are not divided by borough.

TABLE 48

Puerto Rican Students in New York City's Public Schools by School Level, Number of Pupils, and Percent of All Pupils, for 1961, 1965, and 1970

	1961		1965		1970	
	Number	Percent	Number	Percent	Number	Percent
Elementary	106,768	18.6	129,857	21.9	154,917	25.2
Junior high	33,974	18.3	43,833	20.7	52,977	22.8
Academic high	10,914	5.5	24,191	11.4	37,167	15.1
Vocational high	8,755	21.6	11,801	27.8	12,717	32.5
Special schools	1,824	29.1	2,024	30.9	2,262	27.6
All schools	162,235	16.1	211,706	19.8	260,040	22.8

Source: Board of Education of the City of New York, Office of Business Administration, "Annual Census of School Population, October 30, 1970, Summary Tables," Publication No. 340, P.N. S 411, April 1971, Table vii.

TABLE 49

White, Black, and Puerto Rican Family Income, Education
Levels, and Poverty--New York City, 1960 and 1970

	Whites		Blacks		Puerto Ricans	
	1960	1970	1960	1970	1960	1970
Median family income (in dollars)	6,365	10,378	4,437	7,150	3,811	5,575
Percent of gain in real income since 1960	--	26	--	24	--	13
High school graduates (in thousands)	1,620	1,828	199	342	35	69
Percent of adults above age 25 who are high school graduates	40.0	51.0	31.2	40.6	13.0	20.1
College graduates (thousands)	378.9	468.5	26.2	34.5	2.5	3.5
Percent of adults above age 25 who are college graduates (thousands)	9.4	13	4	4	Under 1	1
Individuals below poverty level (thousands)	--	482.5	--	399.0	--	283.0
Percent of population under poverty level	--	8.9	--	24	--	35.1

Source: U.S. Census data cited in New York Times,
August 17, 1972.

TABLE 50

Estimated Median Family Income of Blacks and Puerto Ricans Compared with Whites--New York
City, 1963, 1968, and 1969
(in dollars)

	1963		1968		1969	
	Amount	Percent of Whites	Amount	Percent of Whites	Amount	Percent of Whites
All families	6,130	91.4	8,999	85.4	9,682	87.2
Whites	6,708	100.0	10,538	100.0	11,097	100.0
Blacks	4,333	72.0	7,053	66.9	7,150	64.4
Puerto Rican	3,900	58.1	6,185	58.7	5,575	50.2

Sources: 1963 and 1968 data from Center for Social Research, The Graduate School and University Center, City University of New York, "Estimates of Population Characteristics, New York City, 1964-65-66-68-70," December 1972, Table xxiv, p. 28; 1969 data from 1970 U.S. Census, "General Social and Economic Characteristics, New York," PC(1)-C34 N.Y., Tables 81-101.

TABLE 51

Social and Economic Characteristics of Puerto Ricans in
Long Island, New York, 1970

	Nassau County	Suffolk County
Population	7,224	17,179
Median age	23.1	20.4
Persons under age 18	3,071	7,991
Number of families	1,643	3,567
Percent persons, ages 3 to 34 enrolled in school	54.2	54.1
Males, age 25 and over, school years completed	10.7	10.4
Percent high school graduates	37.1	36.4
Females, age 25 and over, school years completed	11.9	10.5
Percent high school graduates	49.2	38.2
Males, age 16 and over, percent in labor force	85.3	84.6
Percent unemployed	1.7	2.0
Females, age 16 and over, percent in labor force	44.4	41.5
Percent unemployed	6.3	3.8
Median family income (in dollars)	10,534	10,085
Per capita income	2,747	2,315
Percent families under poverty level	10.2	11.3
Percent families receiving public assistance	12.0	10.3

Source: 1970 U.S. Census, "General Social and Economic Characteristics, New York," PC(1)-C34 N.Y., Tables 129-133.

TABLE 52

Comparison of Social and Economic Characteristics for Total
Population, Blacks, and Puerto Ricans in Buffalo, New York SMSA,
1970

	Total	Black	Puerto Rican
Population	1,349,210	108,624	5,532
Percent under age 18	34.4	43.9	55.1
Number of families	337,529	23,571	1,180
Percent enrolled in school, ages 3 to 34	58.5	59.0	54.3
Males, age 25 and over, median school years completed	12.0	9.5	7.0
Percent high school graduates	50.4*	28.6	16.2
Females, age 25 and over, median school years completed	12.0	10.3	8.5
Percent high school graduates	50.4*	32.3	26.8
Males, age 16 and over	436,258	30,050	1,397
Percent in labor force	77.5	69.2	77.1
Percent unemployed	4.4	9.2	9.7
Females, age 16 and over	499,087	35,802	1,276
Percent in labor force	39.8	44.6	33.5
Percent unemployed	5.4	10.8	13.6
Total employed, age 16 and over	509,789	32,963	1,342
Percent professional-technical workers	14.9	7.8	9.6
Median family income (in dollars)	10,430	6,955	6,638
Per capita income (in dollars)	3,363	2,142	1,678
Percent families under poverty level	5.0	24.5	27.1
Percent families receiving public assistance income	6.8	24.2	31.0
Number of households	350,312	26,437	1,197
Percent in owner-occupied units	56.9	15.5	11.6
Mean value of unit (in dollars)	19,776	12,094	11,923
Percent in rental units	43.1	84.5	88.4
Mean gross rent (in dollars)	101	95	92

*One figure provided for both men and women.

Note: The Buffalo SMSA includes surrounding urban areas
such as Lackawanna and Niagara Falls. The total population for
the city of Buffalo alone is 462,781, with 94,336 blacks and
3,880 Puerto Ricans.

Source: 1970 U.S. Census, "General Social and Economic
Characteristics, New York," PC(1)-C34 N.Y., Tables 81-101.

TABLE 53

Population, Age, and Urban Residence for Total Population, Whites, Blacks, and Puerto Ricans in New Jersey, 1970

	Total	White	Black	Puerto Rican Birth or Parentage
Total, state	7,168,164	6,362,337	769,245	135,676
Median age	30.2	31.4	22.9	18.9
Males	3,466,530	3,085,745	363,587	67,534
Median age	28.8	29.8	21.2	18.6
Females	3,701,634	3,276,592	405,658	68,142
Median age	31.5	32.9	24.2	19.2
Percent urban residents	88.9	88.2	94.7	95.9

Sources: 1970 U.S. Census, "General Social and Economic Characteristics, New Jersay," Table 48, p. 32-223, Table 49, p. 32-225.

TABLE 54

New Jersey Cities and Towns with 100 or More Puerto Ricans, 1970

Place	Total Population	Blacks	Puerto Ricans Population	Percent of Population
Asbury Park	16,532	7,044	169	1.0
Atlantic City	47,835	21,014	681	1.4
Bayonne	72,719	3,070	684	0.9
Belleville	34,667	894	195	0.5
Bergenfield	33,267	n.a.	262	0.7
Bloomfield	51,997	823	134	0.2
Bridgeton	20,435	2,731	363	1.7
Camden	102,551	40,128	6,526	6.3
Clifton	82,437	266	374	0.4
Carteret	23,152	775	669	2.8
Cliffside Park	14,024	n.a.	141	1.0
Dover	15,039	n.a.	1,472	9.7
East Orange	75,419	40,110	278	0.3
Elizabeth	112,720	17,389	3,351	2.9
Englewood	25,004	8,208	154	0.6
Fair Lawn	38,029	n.a.	146	0.3
Fort Dix	26,239	4,205	740	2.8
Fort Lee	30,631	n.a.	216	0.7
Freehold	10,545	1,803	128	1.2
Hackensack	35,897	6,008	245	0.6
Hammonton	11,464	n.a.	629	5.4
Harrison	11,800	n.a.	239	2.0
Hoboken	45,390	1,860	10,047	22.1
Irvington	59,727	2,294	802	1.3
Jersey City	260,549	55,005	16,194	6.2
Kearny	37,624	n.a.	147	0.3
Lakewood	17,874	3,456	1,122	6.2
Linden	41,405	5,329	164	0.3
Lodi	25,188	n.a.	441	1.7
Long Branch	31,774	5,210	751	2.3
McGuire A.F.B.	10,933	1,472	126	1.1
Morristown	17,662	3,994	250	1.4
Newark	382,374	207,302	27,443	7.1
New Brunswick	41,862	9,504	1,481	3.5
Old Bridge	25,176	n.a.	358	1.4
Passaic	55,124	9,861	6,826	12.4
Paterson	144,835	38,819	11,927	8.2
Perth Amboy	38,813	2,757	6,606	17.0
Plainfield	46,862	18,745	579	1.2
Pleasantville	13,812	4,563	127	0.9
Rahway	29,102	3,904	207	0.7
Red Bank	12,847	3,228	262	2.0
Sayreville	32,508	n.a.	141	0.4
Somerville	13,652	1,394	306	2.2
Tenafly	14,827	n.a.	132	0.8
Trenton	104,521	39,193	2,932	2.8
Union City	58,537	472	3,114	5.3
Vineland	47,696	3,059	4,734	9.9
West New York	40,666	372	1,167	2.8

Note: "n.a." under column for blacks in some cities indicates that data were not available. Tables used indicated only black populations of 400 persons or more.

Source: 1970 U.S. Census, "General Social and Economic Characteristics, New Jersey," Tables 96-101, 112-116.

TABLE 55

Fertility for Total Population, Whites, Blacks, and Puerto Ricans
in New Jersey, 1970

	All	White	Black	Puerto Rican
Women, 15-24 years old	567,423	439,550	70,827	14,193
Percent ever married	29.8	29.5	31.7	52.3
Number of children born per 1,000 women	286	256	491	790
Women, 25-34 years old	450,650	385,933	60,529	11,786
Percent ever married	88.5	89.5	82.6	94.3
Number of children born per 1,000 women	1,953	1,908	2,269	2,635
Women, 35-44 years old	452,931	400,505	49,225	7,057
Percent ever married	93.6	94.0	90.5	95.6
Number of children born per 1,000 women	2,657	2,617	3,004	3,494

Source: U.S. Census 1970, "General Social and Economic
Characteristics, New Jersey," Table 52, p. NJ 32-231.

TABLE 56

Family Characteristics for Total Population, Whites, Blacks, and
Puerto Ricans in New Jersey, 1970

	All	White	Black	Puerto Rican
Number of families	1,838,809	1,657,936	172,607	29,941
Percent families with own children under age 18	54.8	53.7	65.1	78.6
Percent families with own children under age 6	25.3	24.3	34.4	51.0
Percent families headed by a woman	11.0	9.0	29.6	19.0
Percent families headed by a woman with own children under age 18	50.5	43.0	72.5	85.0
Percent families headed by a woman with own children under age 6	18.8	12.7	36.6	49.4

Source: U.S. Census 1970, "General Social and Economic
Characteristics, New Jersey," Table 48, p. NJ 32-223.

TABLE 57

Years of School Completed for Total Population, Whites, Blacks, and Puerto Ricans in New Jersey, 1970

	Total	White	Black	Puerto Rican
Male 25 years old and over	1,900,387	1,729,099	161,957	25,524
Median school years completed	12.1	12.2	10.2	8.4
Female, 25 years old and over	2,156,219	1,947,635	197,433	25,387
Median school years completed	12.1	12.1	10.7	8.0

Source: 1970 U.S. Census, "General Social and Economic Characteristics, New Jersey," Table 51, p. NJ 32-229.

TABLE 58

Level of School Completed, by Percent of Total Population,
Whites, Blacks, and Puerto Ricans in New Jersey, 1970

	Total	White	Black	Puerto Rican
Persons 25 years old and over	4,056,606	3,676,734	359,390	50,911
Less than 5 years elementary school	4.7	4.3	8.9	23.4
Less than 1 year high school	28.0	27.2	36.0	59.7
4 years high school or more	52.5	54.1	36.2	20.4
4 years college or more	11.8	12.5	4.1	2.0
Median school years completed	12.1	12.1	10.5	8.3
Persons 18-24 years old	720,615	630,555	85,908	19,211
4 years high school or more	66.3	68.0	54.0	28.8
4 years college or more	7.4	8.0	2.0	0.5

Source: 1970 U.S. Census, "General Social and Economic Characteristics, New Jersey," Table 51, p. NJ 32-229.

TABLE 59

School Enrollment by Age Group for Total Population,
Whites, Blacks, and Puerto Ricans in New Jersey, 1970

	Total	White	Black	Puerto Rican
3-34 years old	55.5	56.0	52.5	43.5
3 and 4 years old	14.2	13.5	17.5	7.5
5 and 6 years old	81.1	81.4	78.8	69.4
7-13 years old	98.1	98.4	96.3	93.5
14 and 15 years old	97.1	97.6	93.6	90.1
16 and 17 years old	92.1	93.1	84.7	71.3
18 and 19 years old	58.0	59.9	44.9	37.2
20 and 21 years old	30.8	33.1	14.8	7.3
22-24 years old	13.1	14.0	6.1	3.6
25-34 years old	5.8	6.0	4.4	2.1

Source: 1970 U.S. Census, "General Social and Economic Characteristics, New Jersey," Table 51, p. NJ 32-229.

TABLE 60

Employment Status of White, Black, and Puerto Rican Males
16 to 21 Years Old Not Attending School, New Jersey, 1970

	Total	White	Black	Puerto Rican
Population	115,289	95,964	18,717	4,354
Not high school graduates	44,553	34,376	9,884	3,398
Percent of all males ages 16 to 21	13.3	11.6	25.7	16.2
Employed or in armed forces	28,029	23,189	4,612	2,351
Unemployed or not in labor force	16,524	11,187	5,272	1,047
High school graduate	70,736	61,588	8,833	956
Employed or in armed forces	58,336	51,781	6,293	770
Unemployed or not in labor force	12,400	9,807	2,540	186

Source: 1970 U.S. Census, "General Social and Economic Characteristics, New Jersey," Table 51, p. NJ 32-229.

TABLE 61

Employment Status of Working Age White, Black, and Puerto
Rican Males and Females in New Jersey, 1970

	All	White	Black	Puerto Rican
Males, 16 years and over	2,378,876	2,151,631	215,570	36,871
Percent in labor force	79.6	80.1	74.9	82.1
Percent unemployed	3.1	2.8	6.0	6.0
Females, 16 years and over	2,656,488	2,382,628	259,935	38,133
Percent in labor force	42.5	41.5	51.8	37.1
Percent unemployed	5.0	4.7	7.3	9.9

Source: 1970 U.S. Census, "General Social and Economic Characteristics, New Jersey," Table 53, p. NJ 32-233.

TABLE 62

Income and Poverty Data for White, Black, and Puerto Rican
Families in New Jersey, 1969

	All	White	Black	Puerto Rican
Number of households	1,976,797	1,774,229	193,233	30,610
Median income families and unrelated individuals (in dollars)	9,675	10,157	6,027	5,789
Percent of families receiving public assistance	4.6	3.1	18.3	20.0
Percent of families with income below the poverty line	6.1	4.8	18.9	24.3

Sources: 1970 U.S. Census, "General Social and Economic Characteristics, New Jersey," Table 57, p. NJ 32-
241, Table 58, p. NJ 32-243.

TABLE 63

General Social and Economic Characteristics for Puerto
Ricans in New Jersey, 1960 and 1970

	1960	1970
Population	55,351	135,676
Born in Puerto Rico	39,779	84,257
Born in United States	15,572	51,419
Median age (years)	20.5	18.9
Education		
Males, median school years completed	7.9	8.4
Females, median school years completed	7.7	8.0
Percent of males and females, ages 5 to 34, enrolled in school	38.0	43.5
Employment		
Males, age 14 and older	18,112	39,542
Percent in labor force	84.5	77.1
Percent unemployed	11.5	6.0
Females, age 14 and older	15,742	41,045
Percent in labor force	35.4	34.7
Percent unemployed	13.2	10.1
Income		
Median income of males with income (in dollars)	2,961	5,446
Median income of females with income	1,828	3,557
Median family income*	3,665	6,459

*1960 figure for median family income is for Newark,
since statewide figures were not available.

Source: Various tables of U.S. Census Bureau reports
for 1960 and 1970.

119

TABLE 64

City-by-City Comparison of Key Socioeconomic
Indexes, Puerto Ricans in New Jersey, 1970

Place	Popu-lation	Median Age	School Years (males)	Percent High School Grad-uates
Atlantic City	681	□ 15.2	□ 5.2	15.9
Bayonne	684	19.4	8.5	31.4
Jersey City	16,194	18.8	8.5	15.6
Union City	3,114	22.9	8.3	18.8
Elizabeth	3,351	20.8	8.7	25.2
Irvington	802	18.8	* 9.8	* 33.1
Newark	27,443	16.5	8.0	15.8
Passaic	6,826	20.7	9.1	19.9
Paterson	11,927	18.8	8.1	14.0
Camden	6,526	□ 16.1	□ 6.4	13.5
Trenton	2,932	□ 16.1	7.9	9.8
Vineland	4,734	16.5	6.6	□ 3.3
Clifton	374	* 23.7	* 9.6	* 36.0
Carteret	669	* 24.2	7.7	15.6
Dover	1,472	18.4	7.8	21.4
Hammonton	629	20.3	6.5	8.9
Hoboken	10,047	18.8	7.8	15.5
Lakewood	1,122	20.7	7.0	□ 3.4
Long Branch	751	17.8	8.4	29.8
New Brunswick	1,481	17.6	□ 6.0	□ 2.1
Perth Amboy	6,606	17.7	8.3	15.4
West New York	1,167	* 23.0	* 9.9	* 33.1
Plainfield	578	20.7	8.8	* 35.1

Percent Males in Labor Force	Percent Unemployment	Median Family Income (in dollars)	Per Capita Income (in dollars)	Percent on Public Assistance	Percent Families Under Poverty Level
84.7	* 1.2	□ 3,266	□ 998	15.0	□ 50.6
□ 72.2	4.6	5,750	1,736	19.7	28.2
82.4	6.5	5,476	1,648	20.6	25.1
88.9	□ 11.4	6,676	2,109	9.3	12.9
87.2	4.1	7,665	2,237	10.7	15.6
83.8	4.5	6,781	1,947	15.8	17.5
76.7	6.0	□ 4,983	1,546	□ 29.4	32.8
* 90.3	□ 10.2	5,592	1,836	14.7	26.7
84.3	7.2	5,988	1,812	21.5	22.8
□ 71.9	8.5	5,393	1,419	□ 38.4	□ 35.1
84.3	7.2	6,246	1,611	17.8	25.1
□ 75.8	6.0	5,967	□ 1,466	28.5	27.7
89.3	8.0	* 9,900	* 3,869	* --	* --
89.0	--	7,642	2,350	10.8	17.6
* 94.7	8.2	8,254	1,990	* 4.8	* 11.2
77.8	--	5,604	□ 1,296	23.1	33.1
78.9	6.3	5,346	1,479	21.5	□ 35.8
89.0	3.0	5,655	1,723	□ 37.0	21.5
82.5	□ 11.7	7,248	2,033	9.6	15.4
84.8	7.1	□ 4,817	1,534	28.2	29.9
87.3	2.6	6,853	1,697	16.4	19.4
* 90.1	* 2.4	* 8,369	* 2,421	10.2	* 11.2
86.8	* --	* 8,683	* 2,528	* 2.7	* 7.5

* = Top three or four cities
□ = Bottom three or four cities
-- = "None" or too little to register

Source: 1970 U.S. Census, "General Social and Economic Characteristics, New Jersey," PC(1)-C32, April 1972, Tables 96-101, 112-116.

TABLE 65

Comparison of Socioeconomic Characteristics for Total
Population, Blacks, and Puerto Ricans in Newark, New Jersey, 1970

	All	Black	Puerto Rican
Population, all ages	382,374	207,302	27,443
Percent	100.0	54.2	7.1
Number of families	91,140	46,951	5,974
Percent families with own children under 18	59.0	73.8	80.2
Percent families with female head	26.8	36.4	25.9
Education			
Enrolled in school, ages 3 to 34 years	108,215	67,531	8,238
Percent	50.0	51.7	42.6
Enrolled in high school	24,659	15,270	1,395
Enrolled in college	7,646	3,029	135
Median school years completed, males age 25 and over	9.9	10.1	8.0
Percent high school graduates, males age 25 and over	33.2	31.7	15.8
Median school years completed, women age 25 and over	10.0	10.6	6.9
Percent high school graduates, women age 25 and over	33.2	34.8	11.2
Employment			
Males, age 16 and over	115,247	53,623	6,807
Percent in labor force	74.3	74.6	76.7
Percent unemployed	5.6	7.1	6.0
Females, age 16 and over	137,629	69,015	7,625
Percent in labor force	44.5	46.3	28.6
Percent unemployed	7.8	8.7	14.3
Income			
Median income, families and unrelated individuals (in dollars)	6,191	5,634	4,983
Per capita income	2,498	2,077	1,546
Percent families below poverty line	18.4	23.6	32.8
Percent families that receive public assistance	18.5	26.4	29.4
Housing			
Households	104,791	54,022	6,322
In owner-occupied units	8,841	2,553	136
Mean value per unit (in dollars)	17,969	17,523	13,971
In renter-occupied units	95,950	51,469	6,186
Mean gross rental (in dollars)	113	114	108

Source: 1970 U.S. Census, "General Social and Economic Characteristics, New Jersey," Tables 81-101.

TABLE 66

Comparison of Socioeconomic Characteristics for Total Population, Blacks,
and Puerto Ricans in Jersey City, New Jersey, 1970

	Total	Black	Puerto Rican
Population	206,549	55,005	16,194
Percent	100.0	21.1	6.2
Number of families	65,843	12,208	3,715
Percent families with own children under age 18	51.2	72.6	80.6
Percent families headed by a woman	18.3	31.2	22.8
Education			
Median school years completed, males age 25 and over	10.3	10.1	8.5
Percent high school graduates	35.5*	30.8	15.6
Median school years completed, women age 25 and over	10.3	10.5	8.3
Percent high school graduates	35.5*	32.9	15.6
Employment			
Males, age 16 or more	86,516	14,588	3,991
Percent in labor force	75.5	73.1	82.4
Percent unemployed	3.8	4.8	6.5
Females, age 16 or more	101,879	18,740	4,904
Percent in labor force	43.9	48.5	33.1
Percent unemployed	4.8	6.8	5.5
Selected Professions by Percentage of Workers			
Professional-technical	10.4	6.3	4.4
Managers, administrators	4.7	1.8	2.4
Sales workers	4.9	1.9	4.6
Clerical workers	26.1	20.8	12.8
Craftsmen, foremen	11.0	8.3	10.0
Factory operatives	17.2	24.7	35.2
Transport workers	5.4	7.3	6.8
Laborers (nonfarm)	6.9	9.5	10.4
Services workers	12.0	14.4	13.1
Domestic workers	1.0	3.9	0
Income			
Median income, families and unrelated persons (in dollars)	7,569	5,911	5,476
Per capita income	3,067	2,115	1,648
Percent families living below poverty line	10.3	19.5	25.1
Percent families that receive public assistance	8.1	16.5	20.6
Housing			
Households	71,414	13,225	3,715
In owner-occupied units	8,539	1,159	155
Mean value per unit (in dollars)	17,134	14,317	14,952
In renter-occupied units	62,874	12,066	3,733
Mean gross rental (in dollars)	108	103	95

*Figure is for men and women.

Sources: 1970 U.S. Census, "General Social and Economic Characteristics, New Jersey," Tables 81-101.

TABLE 67

Comparison of Socioeconomic Characteristics for Total Population, Blacks, and Puerto Ricans in Paterson, New
Jersey, 1970

	Total	Black	Puerto Rican
Population	144,835	38,819	11,927
Percent	100.0	26.8	8.2
Number of families	37,070	8,887	2,757
Percent families with own chil-dren under age 18	56.0	72.8	81.5
Percent families headed by a woman	19.1	33.8	21.5
Education			
Median school years completed, males age 25 and over	9.5	9.5	8.1
Percent high school graduates	31.3*	27.1	14.0
Median school years completed, women age 25 and over	9.5	10.3	6.5
Percent high school graudates	31.3*	32.1	14.4
Employment			
Males, age 16 and over	46,409	9,535	3,205
Percent in labor force	77.3	80.6	84.3
Percent unemployed	5.8	7.7	7.2
Females, age 16 and more	54,635	12,349	3,294
Percent in labor force	46.2	51.7	44.3
Percent unemployed	7.7	8.3	13.0
Median income, families and unre-lated persons (in dollars)	7,088	6,047	5,988
Per capita income	2,882	2,097	1,826
Percent families living below poverty line	12.4	21.3	22.8
Percent families that receive public assistance	10.3	21.5	21.5
Housing			
Households	38,466	9,392	2,643
In owner-occupied units	5,956	577	74
Mean value per unit (in dol-lars)	20,965	19,725	n.a.
In renter-occupied units	32,510	8,815	2,569
Mean gross rental (in dollars)	116	121	121

*Only figure available covers both men and women.

Source: 1970 U.S. Census, "General Social and Economic Characteristics, New Jersey," Tables 81-101.

TABLE 68

Comparison of Socioeconomic Characteristics for Total
Population and Puerto Ricans in Hoboken, New Jersey, 1970

	Total	Puerto Rican
Total population	45,390	10,047
Education		
School enrollment, ages 3 to 34	12,670	3,104
Enrolled in high school	2,448	455
Enrolled in college	2,630	90
Percent enrolled in school, ages 3 to 34	52.0	43.4
Median school years, males age 25 and over	8.7	7.8
Percent high school graduates, males	28.0	15.5
Median school years, females age 25 and over	8.7	6.7
Percent high school graduates, females	25.3	11.4
Employment		
Males, age 16 and over	16,297	2,719
Percent in labor force	70.2	78.9
Percent unemployed	5.3	6.3
Females, age 16 and over	16,098	2,935
Percent in labor force	39.5	31.2
Percent unemployed	9.2	11.2
Persons employed, age 16 and above	16,542	2,819
Professional-technical jobs	1,583	59
Dentists and doctors	39	0
Teachers	376	0
Managers and administrators	612	43
Factory operatives	4,448	1,391
Income		
Median income, males age 16 and over (in dollars)	6,343	5,024
Median income, females age 16 and over (in dollars)	4,082	3,470
Median family income (in dollars)	7,786	5,154
Families earning under $1,000 per year	503	195
Families earning over $15,000 per year	1,395	48
Percent families below poverty line	16.9	35.8
Percent families that receive public assistance	9.6	21.5

Source: 1970 U.S. Census, "General Social and Economic Characteristics, New Jersey," Tables 102-116.

TABLE 69

Comparison of Socioeconomic Characteristics for Total
Population, Blacks, and Puerto Ricans in Union City,
New Jersey, 1970

	Total	Black	Puerto Rican
Population	58,537	472	3,114
Percent	100.0	0.8	5.3
Number of families	15,561	131	806
Percent families with own children under 18	49.4	64.9	73.4
Percent families headed by a woman	13.7	1.5	13.6
Education			
Median school years completed, males age 25 and over	9.1	10.0	8.3
Percent high school graduates	30.0*	33.3	18.8
Median school years completed, women age 25 and over	8.8	9.5	8.2
Percent high school graduates	30.0*	40.3	26.0
Employment			
Males, age 16 and over	20,218	185	983
Percent in labor force	79.6	85.9	88.9
Percent unemployed	4.5	10.1	11.4
Females, age 16 and over	23,868	168	961
Percent in labor force	47.9	51.8	44.8
Percent unemployed	8.4	2.2	14.8
Income			
Median income, families and unrelated persons (in dollars)	7,464	8,348	6,676
Per capita income	3,034	2,911	2,109
Percent families below poverty line	10.4	6.9	12.9
Percent families that receive public assistance	7.6	3.8	9.3
Housing			
Households	17,214	140	856
In owner-occupied units	893	0	0
Mean value per unit (in dollars)	18,008	--	--
In renter-occupied units	16,321	140	856
Mean gross rental	115	125	117
Percent households lacking some or all plumbing facilities	6.5	8.6	11.8

*Only figure available includes both men and women.
Source: 1970 U.S. Census, "General Social and Economic Characteristics, New Jersey," Tables 102-116.

TABLE 70

Comparison of Socioeconomic Characteristics for Total
Population, Blacks, and Puerto Ricans in West New York,
New Jersey, 1970

	Total	Black	Puerto Rican
Population	40,666	372	1,167
Percent	100.0	1.0	2.9
Number of families	11,250	102	304
Percent families with own children under age 18	46.7	16.4	76.8
Percent families headed by a woman	13.2	8.9	19.7
Education			
Median school years completed, males age 25 and over	9.1	11.4	9.9
Percent high school graduates	33.9	45.4	33.1
Median school years completed, females age 25 and over	8.8	9.5	8.6
Percent high school graduates	29.4	29.7	14.6
Employment			
Males, age 16 and over	14,234	129	364
Percent in labor force	81.1	81.4	90.1
Percent unemployed	4.5	3.8	2.4
Females, age 16 and over	16,801	152	385
Percent in labor force	50.3	68.4	50.6
Percent unemployed	8.1	13.5	3.2
Income			
Median income, families and unrelated persons (in dollars)	7,988	6,875	8,539
Per capita income	3,377	2,999	2,921
Percent families below poverty line	8.6	3.9	11.2
Percent families that receive public assistance	8.0	5.9	10.2

Source: 1970 U.S. Census, "General Social and Economic Characteristics, New Jersey," Tables 102-116.

TABLE 71

Principal Concentrations and Relative Size of Puerto Rican Populations in Pennsylvania, 1970

City	Total Population	Blacks	Puerto Ricans Population	Percent of Total
Allentown	109,501	1,989	741	0.6
Bethlehem	72,698	1,390	2,966	4.1
Lancaster	57,674	4,249	2,048	3.5
Philadelphia	1,948,608	653,747	26,702	1.4
Reading	87,647	5,524	2,283	2.6
Bristol	12,082	766	570	4.7
Lebanon	28,572	--	687	2.4
West Chester	19,301	3,063	530	2.7

Source: 1970 U.S. Census, "General Social and Economic Characteristics, Pennsylvania," PC(1)-C40 Pa., Tables 81-116.

TABLE 72

Comparison of Socioeconomic Data for Total Population,
Blacks, and Puerto Ricans in Philadelphia, Pennsylvania,
1970

	All	Blacks	Puerto Ricans
Population	4,817,894	843,393	42,696
Born in same state	3,256,189	484,886	14,324
Lived in same house since 1965	2,660,944	400,951	8,312
Education			
Median school years, males age 25 and over	12.0	10.4	8.5
Percent high school graduates	50.6*	36.0	20.4
Median school years, women, age 25 and older	12.0	10.7	7.2
Percent high school graduates	50.6*	36.9	18.4
Employment			
Males, age 16 and over	1,588,229	264,450	11,229
Percent in labor force	78.5	72.4	77.5
Percent unemployed	3.3	6.0	7.7
Females, age 16 and over	1,784,074	297,843	10,719
Percent in labor force	41.8	49.0	34.0
Percent unemployed	4.3	6.5	6.5
Income			
Number of families	1,194,960	188,030	8,817
Median family income (in dollars)	10,783	7,522	6,192
Percent families earning below $1,000 a year	2.0	5.0	8.0
Percent families earning $15,000 or more a year	25.4	7.0	6.5
Percent families below poverty line	7.3	20.7	30.6
Percent families that receive public assistance	28.0	44.7	48.7

*Available figures include men and women together.

Note: Figures encompass the Philadelphia metropolitan area, including adjacent Camden, New Jersey.

Source: 1970 U.S. Census, "General Social and Economic Characteristics, Pennsylvania," PC(1) C40 Pa., Tables 81-101.

TABLE 73

Socioeconomic Characteristics of Puerto Ricans in Connecticut, by Place of Birth, 1970

	Puerto Rican Birth or Parentage	Birth	Parentage
Total population	38,493	24,883	13,610
Family heads	8,580	8,061	519
Children per 1,000 women ever married:			
Women, ages 15 to 24	1,522	1,583	1,114
Women, ages 25 to 34	3,122	3,161	2,447
Women, ages 35 to 44	4,015	4,063	n.a.
Percent enrolled in school, ages 3 to 34 years	46.2	34.4	67.4
Median school years completed	8.2	8.1	11.1
Percent high school graduates	19.2	17.6	42.7
Median family income (in dollars)	6,773	6,683	7,931
Percent of families with income below poverty level	26.1	26.6	17.5
Percent of households in owner-occupied units	12.3	11.6	22.7

Source: 1970 U.S. Census, "Puerto Ricans in the United States," PC(2)-1E, Tables 1-10.

TABLE 74

Comparison of Socioeconomic Data for Total Population and
Puerto Ricans in Boston, Massachusetts, 1970

	Total	Puerto Ricans
Population	641,056	11,321
Number of families	142,019	2,547
Percent enrolled in school, ages 3 to 34	53.9	38.5
Median school years completed, persons age 25 and over	12.1	8.1
Percent high school graduates, persons age 25 and over	53.5	22.5
Males, 16 years and over	212,398	2,982
Percent in labor force	72.0	72.4
Percent unemployed	4.8	11.8
Females, 16 years and over	265,967	2,923
Percent in labor force	47.8	28.7
Percent unemployed	3.7	8.5
Median family income (in dollars)	11,449	4,998
Per capita income (in dollars)	3,713	1,526
Percent families below poverty level	6.1	40.0

Note: Figures given for Boston Standard Metropolitan
Statistical Area (SMSA), which includes the city and surrounding urban areas.

Source: 1970 U.S. Census, "Puerto Ricans in the
United States," PC(2)-1E, various tables.

TABLE 75

Comparison of Socioeconomic Characteristics for Total
Population, Blacks, and Puerto Ricans in Chicago,
Illinois, 1970

	Total	Black	Puerto Rican Birth	Puerto Rican Parentage
Population	6,974,423	1,228,338	53,077	34,091
Number of families	1,733,707	271,297	18,660	650
Percent enrolled in school, ages 3 to 34	54.6	54.6	28.2	72.3
Median school years completed, age 25 and over	12.2	11.0	8.1	8.6
Percent high school graduates, age 25 and over	53.9	39.0	14.2	26.3
Males, age 16 and over	2,285,539	341,385	22,192	1,952
Percent in labor force	80.7	73.1	83.7	63.5
Percent unemployed	3.0	6.3	6.5	11.9
Females, age 16 and over	2,532,813	411,470	20,955	1,952
Percent in labor force	45.2	46.8	40.1	37.4
Percent unemployed	4.1	7.4	9.9	10.8
Median income, males age 16 and over (in dollars)	8,987	6,897	5,478	3,787
Median income, females age 16 and over (in dollars)	4,509	4,488	3,172	2,091
Median family income (in dollars)	11,931	--	7,029	6,750
Per capita income (in dollars)	3,827	2,330	2,754	264
Percent families below poverty level	6.8	19.9	23.4	25.5

Note: Figures are for Chicago Standard Metropolitan
Statistical Area (SMSA), which includes city of Chicago
and surrounding urban areas.

Source: 1970 U.S. Census, "Puerto Ricans in the
United States," PC(2)-1E, various tables.

TABLE 76

Socioeconomic Characteristics of Puerto Ricans in
Cleveland and Lorain, Ohio, 1970

	Cleveland	Lorain
Population	8,104	6,031
Number of families	1,711	1,194
Percent families headed by women	12.1	6.8
Percent enrolled in school, ages 3 to 34	49.9	57.3
Median school years completed, age 25 and over	8.2	7.9
Percent high school graduates, age 25 and over	15.1	14.4
Males, age 16 and over	2,137	1,713
Percent in labor force	85.3	82.5
Percent unemployed	7.6	3.3
Females, age 16 and over	1,925	1,506
Percent in labor force	36.9	28.8
Percent unemployed	4.5	16.2
Median family income (in dollars)	8,118	8,041
Per capita income	1,788	1,939
Percent of families below poverty level	19.9	15.7
Percent families in owner-occupied units	30.0	54.6

Source: 1970 U.S. Census, "Puerto Ricans in the
United States," PC(2)-1E, Tables 14, 16, 30.

KAL WAGENHEIM is a research consultant for the Migration Division of the Puerto Rican government in New York. He is the author of <u>Puerto Rico: A Profile</u> (Praeger, 1970), <u>The Puerto Ricans: Documentary History</u> (Praeger, 1973),and <u>Clemente!</u> (Praeger, 1973).

Mr. Wagenheim lived in Puerto Rico for ten years, during which time he was correspondent for the New York <u>Times</u>, and coeditor of the <u>San Juan Review</u> monthly and the <u>Caribbean Review</u> quarterly. He has also contributed reviews and articles to the <u>New Republic</u>, the <u>Nation</u>, and the <u>New Leader</u>.

RELATED TITLES
Published by
Praeger Special Studies

DESEGREGATING AMERICA'S COLLEGES: A Nationwide
Survey of Black Students, 1972-73
William M. Boyd, II

ETHNIC AND RACIAL SEGREGATION PATTERNS IN
THE NEW YORK METROPOLIS: Residential Patterns
Among White Groups, Blacks, and Puerto Ricans
Nathan Kantrowitz

ETHNIC IDENTITY AND ASSIMILATION: THE POLISH-
AMERICAN COMMUNITY: Case Study of Metropolitan
Los Angeles
Neil C. Sandberg
foreword by Herbert Gans

POLITICAL SOCIALIZATION OF CHICANO CHILDREN:
A Comparative Study with Anglos in California
Schools
Chris F. Garcia

RACIAL TRANSITION IN THE INNER SUBURB:
Studies of the St. Louis Area
edited by
Solomon Sutker and
Sarah Smith Sutker

THE USES OF THE MEDIA BY THE CHICANO
MOVEMENT: A Study of Minority Access
Francisco Lewels, Jr.